SPARK

AGENCY &
PARTNERSHIP LAW

McLaren Legal Publishers LLC
New York

ALSO AVAILABLE IN THIS SERIES:

Agency & Partnership
Antitrust
Bankruptcy
Civil Procedure
Family Law
Federal Income Tax
Labor Law
Wills & Trusts

SPARK LAW SERIES®

AGENCY & PARTNERSHIP LAW

First Edition

John Anderson, Esq.
New York University School of Law

Copyright © 2008 McLaren Legal Publishers LLC

All rights reserved. No part of this book may be reproduced, stored in a retrieval system, or transmitted by any means, electronic, mechanical, photocopying, recording, or otherwise without the express written permission from the Publisher. Copyright is not claimed as to any part of the original work prepared by a United States Government official as part of that person's official duties.

ISBN 10: 0-9801482-0-0
ISBN 13: 978-0-9801482-0-6

Published by
McLaren Legal Publishers LLC
136 West 21st Street, 8th Floor
New York, NY 10011

Web: www.mclarenpublishing.com
Email: contact@mclarenpublishing.com

Printed in the United States of America

Agency & Partnership
SPARK LAW SERIES

HOW TO USE THIS BOOK

This law school study aid is a non-keyed book. While it includes many of the key critical cases in the subject addressed, it is meant to provide an overall rigorous review of the topic indicated and convey key concepts and points of law for general study. For a keyed book linked to a specific casebook, please use our Legal Path Series® of keyed books.

"All of what you need, none of what you don't"

Our law school study guides give you exactly what you need to understand the key principles of the subject, including the sometimes elusive Black Letter law. We are not a replacement for an in depth legal analysis of the subject matter covered; however, we do present what is absolutely critical in a very concise format.

Practice Question & Answer Section

We have included a question and answer section to further test your knowledge of the topics referenced.

Quick Reference Outline

We have included an outline for easy test prep and for quick reference of the material covered.

Agency & Partnership
SPARK LAW SERIES

Abbreviations used in this book

Use of the word "his" in this book is gender neutral and encompasses both "his" and "her."

Pay particular attention to sections with this symbol:

Agency & Partnership
SPARK LAW SERIES

TABLE OF CONTENTS

OVERVIEW OF AGENCY LAW 1
- PURPOSE OF AGENCY LAW 1
- KEY CONCEPTS 1
- BRIEF BACKGROUND 2
- KEY AGENCY RELATIONSHIPS 2
- KEY AGENCY QUESTIONS 3

TORT LIABILITY 4
- INTRODUCTION 4
- MAIN ELEMENTS 4
- THE DOCTRINE OF RESPONDEAT SUPERIOR 5
- MASTER-SERVANT RELATIONSHIP DEFINED 7
- THE MODERN CASE OF FRANCHISES 10
- COURSE OR SCOPE OF EMPLOYMENT 12
- SPECIAL SITUATIONS 13
- DIRECT LIABILITY OF SERVANTS TO THIRD PARTIES 15

CONTRACT LIABILITY 15
- INTRODUCTION 15
- MAIN ELEMENTS 15
- PRINCIPAL-AGENT RELATIONSHIP DEFINED 16
- ACTUAL AUTHORITY 18
- APPARENT AUTHORITY 19
- INHERENT AUTHORITY 22
- RATIFICATION & AFFIRMANCE 25
- LIABILITY OF AGENTS TO THIRD PARTIES FOR CONTRACT 26
- INTRODUCTION 27
- DUTIES OWED BY AGENT TO PRINCIPAL 27
- DUTIES OWED BY PRINCIPAL TO AGENT 31

STEPS IN ANALYSIS OF AN AGENCY LAW ISSUE 32
- PURPOSE OF PARTNERSHIP LAW 33
- KEY CONCEPTS 34
- BRIEF BACKGROUND 35

Agency & Partnership
SPARK LAW SERIES

DEFINING A PARTNERSHIP 39
GENERAL DEFINITION 39
CHARACTERISTICS OF A PARTNERSHIP 39
PARTNERSHIP DISTINGUISHED FROM OTHER BUSINESS RELATIONSHIPS 40

FORMING A PARTNERSHIP 41
BY CONTRACT 41
PARTNERSHIP BY ESTOPPEL 42

FIDUCIARY DUTIES IN PARTNERSHIP 43
DUTY OF LOYALTY 43
DUTY OF CARE 44

RIGHTS OF PARTNERS IN MANAGEMENT & AUTHORITY TO BIND 45
SHARED MANAGEMENT 45
BINDING THE PARTNERSHIP IN CONTRACT 45
BINDING THE PARTNERSHIP IN TORT 46

ENDING A PARTNERSHIP: IN GENERAL 47

ENDING A PARTNERSHIP: DISSOCIATION 48
EVENTS CAUSING DISSOCIATION 48
POWER TO DISSOCIATE 49
CONSEQUENCES OF DISSOCIATION 49

ENDING A PARTNERSHIP: DISSOLUTION 51
EVENTS CAUSING DISSOLUTION 51
JUDICIAL DISSOLUTION 51

QUESTIONS & ANSWERS 53
PROBLEM 1.1: THE FIRM AND ITS AGENTS AND SERVANTS 53
PROBLEM 1.2: THE FIRM AND ITS AGENTS AND SERVANTS 56
PROBLEM 2.1: FIRM'S LIABILITY IN CONTRACT FOR ACTS OF ITS AGENTS 58
PROBLEM 2.2: UNDISCLOSED PRINCIPALS 59
PROBLEM 3.1: CONTRACTS ENTERED INTO BEFORE LLC FORMATION 61
PROBLEM 3.2: FORMATION OF FIRMS 66
PROBLEM 4.1: EXPRESS ACTUAL AUTHORITY 69
PROBLEM 4.2: IMPLIED ACTUAL AUTHORITY 71
PROBLEM 4.3: AGENT'S DUTY OF LOYALTY 74
PROBLEM 5.1: APPARENT AUTHORITY 77

PROBLEM 5.2: ESTOPPEL 80
PROBLEM 8.1: FIRM'S ACCOUNTABILITY (AGENT ISSUES) 108
PROBLEM 15.5: DISSOCIATION OF OWNERS FROM FIRMS 114
PROBLEM 15.7: DISSOCIATION OF OWNERS FROM FIRMS 116

OUTLINE 119

INTRODUCTION TO FIRMS 119
CONTRACTUAL DEALINGS BY AGENTS 135
FORMATION OF FIRMS 141
ACTUAL AUTHORITY OF AGENTS AND ITS CONSEQUENCES 158
POWER OF AGENTS TO BIND THE FIRM BY UNAUTHORIZED ACTS 165
MANAGEMENT AND CONDUCT OF FIRM BUSINESS 169
MANAGERIAL DISCRETION AND FIDUCIARY DUTIES 184
FIRM'S ACCOUNTABILITY FOR
   NOTIFICATION TO AND KNOWLEDGE OF THE AGENT 193
RATIFICATION OF UNAUTHORIZED TRANSACTIONS 200
OWNERSHIP OF THE FIRM 204
DISSOCIATION OF NON-OWNERS 215
DISSOCIATION OF OWNERS FROM FIRMS 227

TABLE OF CASES 243

APPENDIX 245

UNIFORM PARTNERSHIP ACT (1914) 245
REVISED UNIFORM PARTNERSHIP ACT (1997) 252

INDEX 269

Agency & Partnership
SPARK LAW SERIES

OVERVIEW OF AGENCY LAW

Purpose of Agency Law

Agency law defines the rights and liabilities that occur when one party acts on another party's behalf. Because of the number of business transactions that occur based on the use of representation, agency law figures prominently in the commercial context.

An agency relationship is basically a type of contractual relationship that arises through mutual consent between the parties (the principal and her agent). But note, there is no consideration (e.g., payment) needed to support an agency relationship.

Key Concepts

Legal relationship

An agency relationship is a *legal* relationship defined by common law principles. The expressions or actions of each party ultimately determine whether or not a relationship is one of agency, no matter what the parties call the relationship.

Mutual consent

The touchstone of an agency relationship is *mutual consent*. Parties must somehow demonstrate that they intend to be in an agency relationship.

Authority

Authority in agency law is a legal concept distinct from everyday usage of the word authority. Authority may be found to exist even if no outright permission was granted or even if an employee was explicitly instructed to *not* undertake the action in dispute.

Agency & Partnership
SPARK LAW SERIES

Brief Background

Historical Overview of Agency Relationships

The broad concept of agency is a fairly modern development. In early times, a servant was often employed by a household from a young age until death and was, therefore, considered a member of the family. An agent, on the other hand, was only used on an as-needed basis (such as an attorney). Throughout the 19th century, a person performing manual services was considered a servant while a person conducting transactions was considered to be an agent.

As employment structures became more formalized and transactions became more complex, the distinction between an agent and a servant became a matter of degree rather than type. The modern conception is that a servant is a particular type of agent.

Main Source of Law

Because agency law is a common law concept, the relevant legal rules are determined through case-by-case adjudication. Agency law, like contract law, is state law so remember that the legal doctrines which control agency situations may vary from state to state.

Restatement (2d) of Agency

The Restatement of Agency 2d ("Rest. 2d") is a model code of the legal rules, gleaned from case history. Because there is no universal federal law of agency, the Restatement is an excellent source of common agency principles. Many state laws are modeled after the Restatement, and courts often refer to the *Restatement* when giving their reasoning for a particular opinion.

Key Agency Relationships

The first step when faced with an agency issue is to determine what type of relationship exists among the various parties in the dispute. Depending

Agency & Partnership
SPARK LAW SERIES

on the characteristics of the relationship(s), the law will define it as a particular type of agency relationship if applicable.

Principal-Agent Relationship

An agent acts *for* and *in the place of* his principal in conducting transactions. A proper agent has legal authority to act on behalf of his principal.

Example: The manager of one site of a chain retail store may be an agent for the larger company in her interactions with distributors or the like.

Master-Servant Relationship

A master-servant relationship is a specific type of principal-agent relationship. The distinction between a master-servant or a general principal-agent relationship is often a matter of degree. A servant is an agent who not only acts on behalf of his principal but whose physical conduct is *under the control* of his principal.

Example: A store clerk may be a servant of the principal (the owner of the store where he works). The owner has the authority to control the store clerk's physical conduct in regard to the job at hand.

Independent Contractor

An independent contractor is employed by a principal but is *not* authorized to act in the place of the principal to conduct business and is *not under the control* of the principal in how to perform his work.

Example: Subcontractors are usually independent contractors because they determine how they will complete the project on behalf of their clients.

Key Agency Questions

When will an employer be liable for the torts of her employee?

Agency & Partnership
SPARK LAW SERIES

Determining the type of agency relationship that applies in the particular set of circumstances matters because it will bear on the rights and liabilities created as to all parties.

To what extent can an employer be bound to honor a contract made by her employee with third parties? When the principal's identity is known by the third party?

1. When the principal's identity is unknown by the third party?

2. When the principal's very existence is unknown by the third party?

3. What duties do a principal and agent owe one another?

4. How does agency law help business owners control and organize their enterprises?

TORT LIABILITY

Introduction

Tort law covers the situation when one party breaches a duty owed to another party, causing an injury. The victim of a tort will often seek to recover damages for her injuries not only from the actor who actually injured her but also from the party who was "in charge of" that actor.

Agency law determines when an employer will be held liable for the torts of his employee.

Main Elements

Whether an employer will be have to pay for the torts of her employee primarily turns on the *type of relationship* legally established between that employer and her employee.

Agency & Partnership
SPARK LAW SERIES

If the employer and employee have a master-servant relationship, then the master will be liable for the torts of her servant as long as the servant was acting in the *scope of his employment*.

If the employer and employee have an employer-independent contractor relationship, then the employer is usually not liable for the torts of her independent contractor.

Two main elements to find tort liability:

1) a master-servant relationship; and
2) the act occurs during the course or scope of employment.

The Doctrine of Respondeat Superior

Respondeat Superior is the legal doctrine that places the burden of liability on the "master" for the torts of his "servant."

> **This is a doctrine of strict liability because the guilt or innocence of the employer does not matter.**
>
> This is a doctrine of vicarious liability because the employer is taking on the liabilities of someone else, not herself.

The doctrine developed during the medieval period when a servant was considered the property of his or her master. *Respondeat superior* literally means "let the master answer."

Though this rationale no longer applies in today's society, the concept remains that an employer bears responsibility for the acts of her employee in some instances.

Why? Two main reasons:

> 1. Control: If an employer is the one controlling the actions of an employee, then the employer should face the consequences of those actions.
>
> 2. Compensation for victims: Individual employees often do not have the financial resources to fully compensate victims of tort for an

injury. An employer provides a "deeper pocket" to allow full recovery for an innocent victim.

So, if a court finds that a Master-Servant relationship exists, then a tort victim will be allowed to sue the employer as well as the employee under the doctrine of Respondeat Superior.

EXAMPLE:

Policy Chart:
Pros and Cons of finding masters liable for the torts of her servant

Pros for master liability (expanding liability)	Cons for master liability (limiting liability)
Equity: Masters are the ones who profit from the risks taken in business so they should pay for injuries that occur during the course of business	Masters simply pass the costs of liability on to consumers who then have to pay higher prices.
Compensation: companies usually have more money than individual employees; it is unfair if an innocent tort victim cannot be fully compensated for his injury	Compensation is usually too broad anyway, and it is unclear how much damages are really warranted
Deterrence: the threat of liability forces masters to take more precautions (e.g., spend more on training employees, investing in safety measures, etc.)	Lack of information: masters do not have enough information to determine what to spend on precautionary measures even if they bear liability
Masters are the only ones who have the authority to change the way businesses operate	Businesses should be protected from frivolous lawsuits

Agency & Partnership
SPARK LAW SERIES

Master-Servant Relationship Defined

It is best to think about a master-servant relationship as a specific type of principal-agent relationship distinguished by the master's control over the servant's physical conduct.

> Rest. 2d §2: Master; servant; independent contractor
>
> (1): A master is a principal who employs an agent to perform services in his affairs and who controls or has the right to control the physical conduct of the other in the performance of the service.
>
> (2): A servant is an agent employed by a master to perform service in his affairs whose physical conduct in the performance of the services is controlled or is subject to the right to control by the master.

Control over physical conduct

Control over physical conduct does not mean that the master has to physically direct her servant. It means that the master controls or has the right to control *how* the work is to be done, often through detailed instructions or authority over day-to-day actions.

Not all employees are servants. Some employees are either typical agents or independent contractors. Courts consider several factors to distinguish a "regular" employee from a servant or independent contractor:

Factors considered:

1. The agreed upon extent of control which the employer has over the work;

    The greater the amount of control an employer has over her employee, the more likely the relationship is master-servant.

2. Whether the employee is engaged in a distinct occupation or business from that of the employer;

If the employee's work is very different from the business of the employer, then the relationship is more likely an employer-independent contractor.

3. Whether the work is normally supervised or not;

    If the type of work that the employee does is usually done without supervision, then it is more likely that the relationship is employer-independent contractor.

4. Skill required to do the work;

    A higher level of skill usually implies more independence from the employer.

5. Whether the employee or the employer supplies the tools or instrumentalities of the job, and the place where the work is to be completed;

    Employees that supply their own tools or works apart from the employer's place of business are usually independent contractors.

6. Length of time the person is employed;

    Independent contractors are usually employed for short, defined amounts of time whereas agents or servants are usually employed for indefinite amounts of time.

7. Method of payment (e.g., by project or by amount of time);

    Most independent contractors are paid according to each project completed whereas agents or servant employees are usually paid by salaries.

8. Whether the work is part of the regular business of the employer;

    Employees who perform work that is part of the everyday business of the employer are more likely to be agents or servants whereas independent contractors are more likely to be employed for non-frequent purposes.

Agency & Partnership
SPARK LAW SERIES

9. Whether the parties believe they have a master-servant relationship;

10. Whether the principal is or is not in business

(Factors paraphrased from Rest. 2d §220(2))

The issue of day-to-day control:

Humble Oil & Refining Co. v. Martin, 148 Tex. 175, 222 S.W.3d 995 (1949) (liability of oil company for personal injuries caused by gas station personnel)

Humble Oil owned a gas station which it leased to Schneider. Schneider negligently allowed a car to roll off a ramp striking the plaintiff and his two daughters. The issue was whether Humble Oil and Schneider were in a master-servant relationship (if so, Humble would be liable for Schneider's negligence).

Humble and Schneider were found to be in a master-servant relationship because of the following factors:

1) Humble controlled the "details of station work" such as the hours of operation;
2) Humble paid three-fourths of the important operating expenses;
3) there was a strict system of financial control and supervision;
4) Schneider had little or no business discretion;
5) Schneider had to report to Humble on a regular basis;
6) Humble furnished all the station's equipment, advertising, and products;
7) Humble was able to terminate the leasing contract with Schneider at any time.

Hoover v. Sun Oil Company, 58 Del. 553, 212 A.2d 214 (1965) (liability of oil company for personal injuries caused by gas station personnel)

Sun Oil owned a garage which it leased to Barone. A fire was negligently started by an employee of the service station. The injured victim sought damages against the employee, Barone, and Sun Oil. Again, the issue was whether Sun Oil and Barone were in a master-servant relationship.

In this case, Sun Oil and Barone were found to *not* be in a master-servant relationship because:

1) Sun Oil only provided *advice* on how to run the station;
2) Barone was not required to follow Sun Oil's advice;

Agency & Partnership
SPARK LAW SERIES

3) Barone alone assumed the risk of profit or loss for the operation of the business;
4) Barone independently determined the hours of operation and working conditions.

The Modern Case of Franchises

Franchise operations are a popular business model today. A franchisor supplies the franchisee with know-how and strong brand identification, but the franchisee alone usually runs the business just as she would her own small business and bears the risk of profit and loss on her own.

But if a franchisor so controls or regulates the operations of a franchisee's business that the franchisor possesses control within the rules of agency, liability may apply.

Courts seem to have looked to who bears the greater risk of profit or loss rather than day-to-day control in the franchise context. This theory is sometimes called the residual claimant theory, which assigns liability according to the party who bore the risks of profits and losses from the enterprise.

Murphy v. Holiday Inns, Inc., 216 Va. 490, 219 S.E.2d 874 (1975) (whether franchisor liable for negligence of franchisee)

Plaintiff slipped and fell in a Holiday Inn. The issue was whether Holiday Inn and its franchisee were in an agency relationship. The court found no master-servant relationship even though Holiday Inns controlled many of the day-to-day operations such as the standard operating procedures, the training of personnel, and the construction plans of the franchise as well as the conducting of periodic inspections. The court found that the franchise alone ran the risk of profit and loss and, thus, should bear full liability.

Parker v. Domino's Pizza, 629 So.2d 1026 (Fla. Dist. Ct. of Appeal, 4th Dist., 1993) (whether franchisor liable for negligence of franchisee)

Plaintiff was struck by vehicle as a result of negligence on the part of a Domino's franchise employee. The court scrutinized the franchise agreement in order to determine whether the relationship between the franchisor

Agency & Partnership
SPARK LAW SERIES

(Domino's) and the franchisee was that of master-servant or employer-independent contractor.

The court remanded the case suggesting that there was a master-servant relationship because:

1) Domino's franchise manual contained a "prescription for every conceivable facet of business" (e.g., detailed instructions for preparing pizza, maintaining books, advertising, order-taking instructions, etc.)

Policy Chart

Is Day-to-Day Control or Residual Claimant a better rationale for finding tort liability?

Day to Day Control is a better rationale	Residual Claimant is a better rationale
Day to day control serves as a useful proxy for who has the information needed to establish liability.	Most of the time, residual claimants run the operations of a business anyway because they have the most incentive to do so.
Day to day control is fairer because it looks at whose negligence actually caused the accident and does not discourage enterprise.	Residual claimant is fairer because residual claimants are the ones who benefit from risk taking so they should pay when those risks cause injury.
Enterprise liability (i.e., residual claimant theory) does not distinguish between employers who could have prevented the injury and those who could not have. Such a rule is therefore arbitrary.	

Agency & Partnership
SPARK LAW SERIES

Course or Scope of Employment

Even if a master-servant relationship exists, a master will only be held liable for the acts committed by her servant if the act occurs during the *course or scope* of the servant's employment.

> *Rest. 2d §219: When Master is Liable for Torts of His Servants*
>
> *(1): A master is liable for the torts of his servants committed while acting in the scope of their employment*
>
>> **Basically, scope of employment means that the employee must have been doing what he was employed to do during his working hours at the time that the negligence occurred.**
>
> *Rest. 2d §229: Kind of Conduct within Scope of Employment*
>
> *(1) To be within the scope of the employment, conduct must be of the same general nature as that authorized, or incidental to the conduct authorized.*

If an act was not explicitly authorized, then the following factors are considered in determining whether a particular act will nonetheless be considered as occurring within the scope of employment:

1) whether the act is one commonly done by such employees;
2) the time, place, and purpose of the act;
3) whether the act ever occurred in previous situations;
4) the extent to which the employer's interests were advanced by the act;
5) whether the act was authorized to any other servants;
6) whether the employer had reason to know that the servant would be acting in the manner in question;
7) the similarity between the unauthorized act and authorized acts;
8) whether the employer furnished the means or tools by which the injury was inflicted (e.g., company car);
9) the extent that the act departs from the normal methods of business;
10) whether the act involved the commission of a serious crime.

> *(Paraphrased from Rest. 2d §229(2)).*

Agency & Partnership
SPARK LAW SERIES

Thus, even acts that are specifically forbidden by the employer may be found to be within the scope of employment if they qualify under the listed factors.

Special Situations

Acts outside the Scope of Employment

Courts have found employers liable for the torts of servants acting outside the scope of employment in certain specific situations:

(a) where the employer nevertheless intended the conduct or the consequences of the conduct;

(b) where the employer was negligent or reckless herself;

(c) where the employer has a non-delegable duty;

(d) where the servant purported to act on behalf of the principal and there was reliance by the third party on this apparent authority; and

(e) the servant was aided in accomplishing the tort by the agency relationship.

EXAMPLE: A boss fires a foreman whose job had been to direct others to cut down trees. Before others know about the discharge, the foreman tells his crew to cut down the trees on B's property. The boss will be liable to B for the trespass.

Apparent authority in tort:

Billops v. Magness Construction Co., 391 A.2d 196 (Del. Sup. 1978) (franchise case where court relies on apparent authority to find tort liability)

Court finds that people's reliance on brand names such as Hilton Hotels creates an apparent authority; thereby a franchisor is found liable in a tort action. Even though no master-servant agency relationship found, the elements of apparent authority combined with detrimental reliance create liability.

Agency & Partnership
SPARK LAW SERIES

Intentional Torts

An employer may be found liable under respondeat superior for even the intentional torts of her servant if the tort occurred within the scope of his employment.

The key question will be whether the servant was motivated by personal reasons or by a desire to further his employer's business. Because most employers are not in the business to commit an intentional tort, the more serious the act, the less likely it will be found to be within the scope of employment.

Crimes

Respondeat superior only applies to civil liability. So, an employer will usually not be held liable for the criminal acts of her servant.

There are only a couple exceptions to this criminal liability, not based on agency principles:

> 1) When the employer has a duty of utmost care, such as a common carrier

> The duty of utmost care makes businesses such as railroads and airlines liable for *any* tort or criminal acts of their employees committed against customers.

> 2) Defamation

> If a servant is employed to make statements on behalf of an employer, the employer may be held liable for false statements made even if the servant is not motivated to serve the employer in making those statements.

> *Rest. 2d. §247: Defamation*
> *A master is subject to liability for defamatory statements made by a servant acting within the scope of his employment, or, as to those hearing or reading the statement, within his apparent authority.*

Example: A newspaper editor employed by a corporation publishes libelous remarks about a 3rd party just to hurt the corporation. The corporation will nonetheless be held liable to the 3rd party for the defamation.

Direct Liability of Servants to Third Parties

Just because you are an agent at the time you commit a tort does not mean that you yourself will not be liable for that tort. An actual tortfeasor is always liable for his own conduct. A tort victim, therefore, typically sues the employee *as well as his* employer. Because of the limited assets of most individuals, a tort victim seeking complete recovery for his injuries will want to name as many defendants as possible.

CONTRACT LIABILITY

Introduction

Business agreements occur based on trusted representations on a regular basis. Laws of agency determine in what instances it is best to bind the employer for valid contracts made by an employee *even if* the employer had no knowledge that such a contract was being made. Without such laws, it would arguably be more difficult and costly to transact business quickly and efficiently.

Most contract disputes arise when an agent makes a contract with a third party on the principal's behalf which the principal later refuses to honor. The principal in this situation will argue that the agent did not have the right to enter into that contract. Third parties will then seek to enforce the contract by "binding" the principal to the contract through the legal doctrines of agency.

Main Elements

As in tort, courts will first look to the type of relationship that exists between the employer and employee. Namely, the court will determine whether a *principal-agent relationship* exists.

Agency & Partnership
SPARK LAW SERIES

The court will then turn to what *authority* the agent possessed to engage in such contracts. Because a principal-agent relationship is rarely contested, the real question for the court will usually be the determination of authority.

Finally, the grieving party must show *reliance* on a certain set of reasonable beliefs based on the demonstrated principal-agent relationship in order to support a cause of action.

Three main elements to find contract liability:

1) a principal-agent relationship;
2) authority; and
3) reliance upon that authority.

Principal-Agent Relationship Defined

A principal-agent relationship is created when an A (agent) acts on behalf of a P (principal) subject to the P's control, with both A and P having demonstrated consent to this arrangement.

> **Rest. 2d §1: Agency; Principal; Agent**
>
> **(1) Agency is the fiduciary relationship which results from the manifestation of consent by one person to another that the other shall act on his behalf and subject to his control, and consent by the other so to act.**
> **(2) The one for whom action is to be taken is the principal.**
> **(3) The one who is to act is the agent.**

Key Concepts

Agency is a *fiduciary relationship*, meaning it is based on trust and duty between principal and agent.

Agents act on behalf and in place of the principal. A person who acts for his own interests (e.g., makes his own contract with a third party) is not an agent in that transaction.

Agency & Partnership
SPARK LAW SERIES

The creation of an agency relationship turns on a *manifestation of consent*. Consent can be manifest in express or implied ways. For example, a signed contract of employment is an express manifestation of consent that an employer and employee agree to be in a principal-agent relationship. Consent may also be *implied* from certain actions by either party or from the circumstances surrounding the relationship.

EXAMPLE: A signed contract of employment is an express manifestation of consent that an employer and employee agree to be in a principal-agent relationship.

Example: A manufacturer habitually leaves his products with a broker. The leaving of products in and of itself is an implied manifestation of consent that the manufacturer and broker agree to be in a principal-agent relationship.

Types of Agents

There are two types of agents:

Special Agents: The agent is only an agent for a particular act or transaction.

General Agents: All other agents besides special agents are general agents.

Agency & Partnership
SPARK LAW SERIES

TYPES OF PRINCIPALS

There are three types of principals:

1. <u>Disclosed Principals</u>: The existence and identity of the principal is known by the third party.

2. <u>Partially Disclosed Principal</u>: The existence of a principal is known but not the exact identity of that principal.

3. <u>Undisclosed Principal</u>: The very existence of a principal is unknown.

Types of Authority

There are three main types of authority. A principal can be bound to the contracts her agent makes with third parties if there is one of the following types of authority:

Actual Authority – when a principal acts in such a way toward her agent that the agent reasonably believes that the principal wants the agent to enter into such a contract

Apparent Authority – when a principal acts in such a way towards a third party which gives the impression that the principal's agent has the power to enter into such a contract with that third party

Inherent Authority – when it is typical for an agent in a similar position to have the power to enter into such a contact.

Actual Authority

Actual authority occurs when the principal manifests consent *to the agent* that the agent should enter into such a contract. This doctrine looks at the situation from the point of view of the agent.

Agency & Partnership
SPARK LAW SERIES

A principal's consent can be manifest to the agent by express methods of the principal (such as a signed contract) or by implied methods of the principal (such as oral statements).

The conduct of the principal must be reasonably interpreted by the agent as to have given him the authority in question. As you can imagine, reasonable belief comes more into question for implicit acts of consent by the principal.

Additionally, the agent must have *relied* upon this reasonable belief in engaging in the disputed contract.

Rest. 2d §7: Authority

[Actual] authority is the power of the agent to affect the legal relations of the principal by acts done in accordance with the principal's manifestations of consent to him.

Rest. 2d §26: Creation of Authority; General Rule

[Actual] authority to do an act can be created by written or spoken words or other conduct of the principal which, reasonably interpreted, causes the agent to believe that the principal desires him so to act on the principal's account.

Mill Street Church of Christ v. Hogan, 785 S.W.2d 263 (Ky. 1990)

A church hired one of its members, Bill, to paint the church building. Bill hired his brother Sam to assist him. (Bill had been hired to do similar jobs in the past and had hired Sam to help him in the past.) Bill did not know that the church had chosen another person to help Bill in the painting job. When Sam sought worker's compensation for falling and breaking his arm while on the job, the church claimed that Bill did not have authority to hire Sam.

The court found that Bill had implied actual authority to hire Sam.

Apparent Authority

Apparent authority occurs when the principal manifests consent through her actions to *third parties*. This doctrine looks at the situation from the point of view of the third party.

Agency & Partnership
SPARK LAW SERIES

Apparent authority can be created by written or spoken words or by any other conduct of the principal which is reasonably interpreted by a third person to mean that the agent has the consent of the principal.

Because some sort of interaction between the principal and third party is needed to establish apparent authority, this doctrine never applies in the case of an undisclosed principal.

> **Rest. 2d §8: Apparent Authority**
> Apparent authority is the power to affect the legal relations of another person by transactions with third persons, professedly as agent for the other, arising from and in accordance with the other's manifestations to such third persons.

> **Rest. 2d §27: Creation of Apparent Authority**
> [A]pparent authority to do an act is created as to a third person by written or spoken words or any other conduct of the principal which, reasonably interpreted, causes the third person to believe that the principal consents to have the act done on his behalf by the person purporting to act for him.

To establish a claim based on apparent authority, plaintiff must show:

1) reasonable belief that such authority existed based on the principal's conduct, and
2) reliance on the fact that such authority existed.

Lind v. Schenley Industries, Inc., 278 F.2d 79 (3d Cir. 1960) (en banc) (will a boss be held to a contract he never agreed to)

Plaintiff moved to another city because his direct boss told him that he would be paid 1% commission on total sales. The principal (upper-level boss) did not know the terms of this contract and refused to pay plaintiff this commission upon learning about the exact terms.

Agency & Partnership
SPARK LAW SERIES

Factors identified to find apparent authority:

1) Principal had given instructions to plaintiff to negotiate the terms of a new contract with his direct boss. *Relevant element: Conduct of the Principal*
2) The terms conveyed to plaintiff were *reasonably believable* even though the new salary would supersede that of the plaintiff's direct boss. *Relevant element: Reasonable Belief*
3) Plaintiff relied upon this reasonable belief, to his detriment. *Relevant element: Reliance*

Policy Chart
Arguments For and Against Apparent Authority

FOR APPARENT AUTHORITY	AGAINST APPARENT AUTHORITY
Cuts down the transaction costs of third parties having to confirm that representations are reliable	Too broad and malleable of a concept increases the overall costs of all transactions
Because the principal controls all the evidence of having given the agent proper authority, it's more fair to analyze situations from the agent's point of view	Encourages frivolous litigation because a deeper pocket is available
Third parties should be able to rely on contracts made with agents more often than not	Prices of contracts can be adjusted to account for any uncertainty
Employees are already deterred from forming unauthorized contracts by the threat of discharge so apparent authority is an accurate barometer of appropriate contracts	Unfair for companies to pay for unauthorized behavior of agents

Agency & Partnership
SPARK LAW SERIES

| Forces the principal to be clear and cautious in her actions and helps prevent misunderstandings | Slows down the ability of businesses to freely and efficiently transact |

Inherent Authority

Inherent authority occurs when an agent acts in a typical manner as similar agents. Inherent authority is created simply by the act or contract entered into by the agent – even if expressly forbidden by the principal. It has been suggested that the doctrine looks at the situation from the point of view of the *principal* in that this authority covers the types of acts which are reasonably foreseeable by the very existence of an agency relationship.

Inherent authority is the authority that is typical for an agent in a similar position to have. An agent who acts with inherent authority binds his principal in actions done on the principal's behalf as long as such action is *usual or necessary*.

The only way by which an *undisclosed principal* will be bound to a disputed contract made by her agent is through the doctrine of inherent authority.

Inherent authority is more conceptual than the other types of authority and only applies in very rare situations. **It is best to think about inherent authority as a last resort:** first look to see if there is actual or apparent authority or a basis in general contract law. Inherent authority has not been explicitly recognized by a majority of states but is codified in the Restatement (2nd) of Agency, and no court has ever directly repudiated the theory.

> *Rest. 2d §8A: Inherent Agency Power*
>
> *Inherent agency [authority] is a term used in the restatement of this subject to indicate the power of an agent which is derived not from authority, apparent authority or estoppel, but **solely from the agency relation** and exists for the protection of persons harmed by or dealing with a servant or other agent. (emphasis added)*

Agency & Partnership
SPARK LAW SERIES

Rest. 2d §195: Acts of Manager Appearing to be Owner
An undisclosed principal who entrusts an agent with the management of his business is subject to liability to third persons with whom the agent enters into transactions usual in such businesses and on the principal's account, although contrary to the directions of the principal.

Rest. 2d §161: Unauthorized Acts of General Agent

A general agent for a disclosed or partially disclosed principal subjects his principal to liability for acts done on his account which usually accompany or are incidental to transactions which the agent is authorized to conduct if, although they are forbidden by the principal, the other party [1] reasonably believes that the agent is authorized to do them, and [2] has no notice that he is not so authorized.

Watteau v. Fenwick, 1 Queens Bench 346 (1892)
Manager of a pub with his name of the door had sold the pub to an undisclosed principal but remained as manager. He entered into unauthorized contracts (to buy cigars, not just water and ale) with distributors as if he was still the owner, and the principal was undisclosed.

The court found the principal liable for the contracts entered into by the manager even though they were against the principal's express instructions.

Kidd v. Thomas A. Edison, Inc., 239 Fed. 405 (S.D.N.Y. 1917) (Hand, J.)

Fuller was an agent of the defendant who had contracted with Kidd to perform a series of recorded singing recitals. Kidd alleged that the contract was an unconditional engagement for a full singing tour while the defendant alleged that Fuller had no authority to do so.

The court found that the customary powers of agents like Fuller had no limitations. *Note: the opinion uses the term "apparent authority" but as no manifestations were made by the defendant to the plaintiff, inherent authority correctly applies.*

Agency & Partnership
SPARK LAW SERIES

Nogales Service Center v. Atlantic Richfield Co., 613 P.2d 293 (1980)

A manager of ARCO's truck stop marketing division enters into an agreement with Nogales that ARCO will sell gas to him at lower prices. The defendant objected to separate jury instructions about inherent authority claiming that the provisions were already covered in instructions on apparent authority.

The court affirmed the jury instructions thus clearly validating the use of inherent authority as a separate basis of liability from actual or apparent authority.

Types of situations in which inherent authority occurs:

1) general agent does something similar to what he's authorized to do, but in violation of express orders by principal;
2) agent enters into a transaction purely for his own purposes but the transaction would be authorized if he acted with the proper motive of benefiting the principal;
3) agent is authorized to dispose of goods and uses an unauthorized method of disposal

Policy Chart
Arguments For and Against Inherent Authority

FOR INHERENT AUTHORITY	AGAINST INHERENT AUTHORITY
Allows third parties to be fully compensated for wrongdoing	Windfall for third party created and price increases for contracts and goods incentivized.
Risk of loss should fall on the principal rather than the third party	Third party should ask more questions during dealings to find if there is a principal in existence

Agency & Partnership
SPARK LAW SERIES

Review Chart: Types of Authority

Principal's Conduct toward the Agent	Principal's Conduct towards the Third Party	Available Type(s) of Authority
Express/implied consent	None	Actual Authority
None	Express/implied consent	Apparent Authority
None	None	Inherent Authority

The types of authority are all *independent* of and *do not conflict* with one another. This means that one situation can have elements of all three types of authority, two of the three types of authority, or just one type of authority. **It only takes one type of authority to be established in order to bind the principal to the contract of her agent.**

Ratification & Affirmance

Even if no actual, apparent, or inherent authority is found to exist at the time of the agent's action, if the principal acts in a manner which expresses or implies that she authorizes the contract *after the fact*, the principal will then be bound by ratification.

The principal's conduct which signals an after-the-fact authorization is called *affirmance*; affirmance results in *ratification* of the previously-unauthorized action or contract.

Rest. 2d §82: Ratification

Ratification is the affirmance by a person of a prior act which did not bind him but which was done or professedly done on his account, whereby the act, as to some or all persons, is given effect as if originally authorized by him.

Agency & Partnership
SPARK LAW SERIES

Rest. 2d §83: Affirmance
Affirmance is either

(a) a manifestation of an election by one on whose account an unauthorized act has been done to treat the act as authorized, or
(b) conduct by him justifiable only if there were such an election.

Types of conduct which could be considered affirmance:

1) receiving or retaining property based on the validity of the disputed contract;
2) maintaining or defending against an action based on the validity of the disputed contract;
3) in some circumstances, silence can serve as an affirmance.

The justification for ratification through affirmance is that principals should not receive benefits from acting as if a contract is valid (even if it really is invalid) without also accepting responsibility for the validity of the contract.

Example: Without any authority, A contracts to sell property to T on P's behalf. Based on this, T approaches P and offers the money for the property. If P accepts this money, he will be held to have affirmed A's conduct, resulting in ratification of the contract.

Liability of Agents to Third Parties for Contract

The liability of agents themselves depends on the type of principal involved in the transaction.

If a *disclosed principal* is at issue, then the *agent is not party* to the contract and, therefore, cannot be held liable for the contract terms.

If a *partially disclosed principal* is at issue, then the *agent is party* to the contract unless otherwise agreed.

If an *undisclosed principal* is at issue, then the *agent is party* to the contract.

Agency & Partnership
SPARK LAW SERIES

FIDUCIARY DUTIES IN AGENCY

Introduction

Agency is both a consensual and a fiduciary relationship. A principal-agent relationship, like any contractual relationship, necessarily encompasses a set of duties to one another. The primary source for the duties owed between and among principals, agents, and third parties is from the formation of a **contract**.

But the agency relationship is not an arms-length contract between two parties who are unfamiliar to each other. The principal-agent relationship is an intimate one where the agent functions as a fiduciary for his principal.

As a fiduciary relationship, the agent owes particular duties to his principal beyond the contract. In particular, the duty of loyalty an agent owes his principal is what distinguishes the agency relationship from a typical contractual relationship.

Duties Owed by Agent to Principal

Agents are first and foremost bounds to the terms they agreed to through their contract with a principal, if applicable.

> Rest. 2d §376: Effect of Manifestations of Consent between Principal and Agent – General Rule
>
> The existence and extent of the duties of the agent to the principal are determined by the terms of the agreement between the parties, interpreted in light of the circumstances under which it is made, except to the extent that fraud, duress, illegality, or the incapacity of one or both of the parties to the agreement modifies it or deprives it of legal effect.

> **Duties of Loyalty**
> Because an agent is a fiduciary, he owes a duty to be loyal to his principal on all matters connected with the agency relationship.

Agency & Partnership
SPARK LAW SERIES

Rest. 2d §387: Duties of Loyalty – General Principle

Unless otherwise agreed, an agent is subject to a duty to act solely for the benefit of the principal in all matters connected with his agency.

Examples of Duties of Loyalty:

- **Duty Not To Use Confidential Information**

An agent is not to use information confidentially given to him by the principal or otherwise acquired during the course of the agency relationship to compete or injure the principal. .(See Rest. 2d §395)

After the agency relationship is over, the former agent continues to have a duty to not use trade secrets, customer lists, or similar confidential information. The agent may use any *general* information acquired while he was working as an agent.

- **Duty to Account for Profits**

An agent is not to make secret profits from contracts entered into as a result of the agency relationship without sharing them with the principal.

General Automotive Mfg. Co. v. Singer, 19 Wis. 2d 528, 120 N.W. 2d 659 (1963) (mechanic referring customers)

Singer was a mechanic at a garage owned by GM. He referred some customers to other garages and got a commission from these referrals. Singer claims he only referred customers to other garages when the GM garage was not well-suited for the job.

The court held that Singer violated the duty of loyalty to disclose secret profits. The commission he charged for the referrals gave him an incentive to aid businesses directly adverse to his principal.

Agency & Partnership
SPARK LAW SERIES

- **Duty to Not Act as an Adverse Party**

An agent is not to deal with his principal as an adverse party in any transaction that is part of the agency relationship without the knowledge of his principal.

- **Duty to Not Compete**

An agent is not to compete with his principal in the area covered by the agency relationship during the time of that relationship.

An agent can prepare to compete before the agency relationship ends but cannot solicit customers for a rival business nor otherwise directly compete while still an agent.

Example: A manager for P's business can purchase a rival business before the end of his employment period but cannot recruit customers for that competing business while he's still employed by P.

Bancroft-Whitney Co. v. Glen, 411 P. 2d 921, 49 Cal. Rptr. 825 (1966)

Agent violated his fiduciary duty to his principal by arranging and soliciting employees below him to go to a competing office with him. Agent used inside information to make better offers to those employees he particularly wanted to recruit and also misled the principal about the oncoming raid of employees.

Agent breached duty by 1) not disclosing information to his principal that would prevent injury to the principal, and 2) using insider information to directly compete with the principal. The course of conduct amounted to a breach of the fiduciary duties owed as an agent to his principal.

<u>Agents cannot</u>:

1) use confidential information peculiar to the principal's business and acquired through the agency relationship;
2) solicit for customers for a competitor while employed; or
3) solicit other employees to join competitor while employed.

Agency & Partnership
SPARK LAW SERIES

Duty of Care

There is an implied duty in every agency agreement that the agent will use reasonable care, diligence, and skill in his work for the principal.

> *Rest. 2d §379: Duty of Care and Skill*
> *Unless otherwise agreed, a paid agent is subject to a duty to the principal to act with standard care and with the skill which is standard in the locality for the kind of work which he is employed to perform . . .*

Policy Chart:

Pros and Cons of Fiduciary Duties as Default Terms of Contracts

Pros: FDs as default terms	**Cons**: FDs as default terms
Cuts contracting costs by not having to negotiate every single term of an agency contract; impossible to contract for every possible contingency anyway so default terms make sense	Default terms encourage parties to not read their contracts and remain unsophisticated in their negotiations
Contract terms are often difficult to interpret whereas default terms have accepted meanings	Parties should have freedom of choice in determining the terms of their agreement
Default terms cover what most parties would want anyway; obviates need to "reinvent the wheel" with each contract	Risk that unwanted terms will be included if default terms are used
The fairness of default terms has been refined by courts for many years	Using default terms stifles innovation in the methods of transacting business
Having to always negotiate a contract discourages employment	Parties themselves know best what exactly they want in their contract

Agency & Partnership
SPARK LAW SERIES

Default terms protect unsophisticated parties who may not be as familiar with contingences	Parties generally lack information as to what the default terms are; contracting protects unsophisticated parties because all terms are discussed
Default terms account for the fact that most principals are better informed than agent and thereby protect inexperienced agents	Default terms are unfair to start with as they mostly cover the duties an agent has to his principal
Default terms are expeditious	Default terms are paternalistic

Duties Owed by Principal to Agent

Like agents, principals are first and foremost bound to any duties in the agency contract. Beyond those duties, there are also certain duties implied in every agency relationship.

Duty to Compensate

Unless there is reason to believe that the agent's services are intended to be gratuitous, a principal must compensate the agent for the agreed-upon value of those services.

Duty to Indemnify

In the absence of terms to the contrary, a principal has a duty to indemnify her agent where the agent

a) makes a payment authorized or made necessary in executing principal's affairs or otherwise beneficial to the principal; or
b) suffers a loss which, because of the agency relationship, is fair for the principal to bear.

There is no duty on the principal to indemnify the agent for:

a) loss or other harm arising from unauthorized acts of the agent that do not benefit the principal;
b) loss or other harm arising solely from negligence of the agent;

Agency & Partnership
SPARK LAW SERIES

c) physical harm from the performance of authorized acts, torts, or lawsuits against the agent; or

d) loss from an enterprise which the agent knew to be illegal.

STEPS IN ANALYSIS OF AN AGENCY LAW ISSUE

1. Identify the act at issue

    Is it a tort or a contract?

2. Identify the legal relationships among all parties

    Is there a principal-agent relationship?
    Is there a master-servant relationship?

3. Identify the relevant legal rules based on the act and legal relationship

    If there is a principal-agent relationship at issue, what type of authority is present?

    If there is a master-servant relationship at issue, was the servant acting within the scope of employment?

Agency & Partnership
SPARK LAW SERIES

OVERVIEW OF PARTNERSHIP LAW

Purpose of Partnership Law

Partnership law defines the rights and liabilities that occur when two or more parties carry on a business relationship with "partnership" characteristics (e.g., co-ownership, profit sharing). No official documents need to be filed to form a general partnership (unlike a corporation) so a partnership can arise as a default legal relationship.

Partnership law is similar to agency law in many respects. Conceptually, a partner is considered an agent for her co-partners in acts and purposes within the scope of the partnership relationship. The fiduciary duties partners owe one another also draw from their status as agents for each other and for the partnership.

Forming a partnership solves three main problems for businesses:

1) The Principal-Agent Problem
   There is not as much need for regulation over a partner's behavior as over an employee's behavior because a partner has stronger incentives to benefit the partnership.

2) Relationships with Third Parties
   Relationships with third parties are more efficient and trustworthy as the sharing of both risks and benefits in such relations is unquestioned and the liabilities are more straightforward.

3) Organizational Control

   Partnerships can be an excellent way to share the responsibilities and duties of running a business and can allow businesses to run more efficiently.

A common reason for a business to form a partnership instead of a corporation is the substantial tax advantages (corporations are subject to a sort of "double taxation" while partnerships are not).

Another reason is that, historically, certain types of professionals (including lawyers) going into business together were not allowed to form corporations

Agency & Partnership
SPARK LAW SERIES

because the liability shield given to corporations was considered inappropriate given the nature of the client relationship. Today, most states allow professionals to form limited liability partnerships ("LLPs") which are partnerships that feature the liability shield of a corporation. LLPs are discussed below in "Types of Partnerships."

Key Concepts

1. Consensual relationship

A partnership relationship is a legal relationship that is formed whenever two or more persons agree to go into business together according to certain partnership characteristics.

This agreement need not be as explicit as naming the enterprise a "partnership." As in agency law, the expressions and actions of each party ultimately determine whether or not a partnership exists, no matter what the parties call the relationship. Also, as in agency, a general partnership is a default relationship that even arises in the absence of a partnership agreement as long as certain characteristics exist.

2. Fiduciary Duties

Each partner functions as an agent for each other partner as well as for the partnership as a whole. Therefore, fiduciary duties are owed among all partners and between the partner and the partnership.

3. Liability

Contract Liability: Every partner (acting as an agent) has the power to bind the entire partnership under actual, apparent, or inherent authority when forming contracts that have to do with the partnership business.

Tort Liability: The partnership as a whole as well as every partner individually is liable for the torts of each fellow partner.

Agency & Partnership
SPARK LAW SERIES

Brief Background

    4.   Development of Partnership Law

Partnerships have always been a popular method of doing business. Along with sole proprietorships, partnerships (where there is more than one "owner" of a business) characterize the bulk of small business entities.

Partnerships can range from two to hundreds of partners all conducting a business enterprise together. The more partners or the more complex a business operation becomes, the more likely the owners will decide to form a corporation.

In common law, a partnership was merely considered an aggregate of individuals who were working together for a common goal. This "aggregate" theory of a partnership explains why an action at common law could not be brought against a partnership as an entity; each individual partner had to be named in a suit. Similarly, at common law, real property could not be owned by the partnership itself. Property was instead owned by the partners as individuals.

Today, partnerships are mostly considered a separate entity from the individuals who comprise it. So, a partnership may own property, transact business, and be brought to court as an entity separate from the individual partners. Only for purposes of joint and several liability and for certain tax purposes is the partnership an aggregate of individuals.

The UPA (discussed below) generally follows the "aggregate" theory of partnership but the more modern RUPA (also discussed below) explicitly follows the "entity" theory.

> RUPA § 201: *Partnership as Entity*
> *A partnership is an entity distinct from its partners.*

Agency & Partnership
SPARK LAW SERIES

5. Types of Partnerships

    General Partnership ("GP")

    This is the archetypal partnership relationship and the only type of partnership that can be formed by default. Partnership law mainly concerns GPs because other types of partnerships (discussed below) usually have a contract which governs the details of the partnership relationship. Partnership law works to provide guidance for partnership relationships formed in the absence of contract and, therefore, applies most often in the case of GPs.

    Limited Liability Partnership ("LLP")

    Limited liability partnerships ("LLP"s) are a modern conception. An LLP is basically a general partnership that features a partial shield from liability. Unlike GPs, there is no way that an LLP can arise by default. To form an LLP, formal registration must be filed with the appropriate public official.

    This registration process will ask the proposed LLP to disclose certain information. The nature of this information varies from state to state but can include things such as address of the business, number of partners, statement of partnership's purpose, and statement of insurance.

    Limited Partnership

    Limited partnerships, unlike GPs and like LLPs, can only be formed by observing certain formalities (namely, filing with the appropriate public official).

    A limited partnership is comprised of two types of partners: 1) general partners, and 2) limited partners. A limited partnership must have at least one of each type of partner. General partners are typical partners who contribute capital, share in profits and losses, and probably participate in managing the business. Limited partners, in contrast, are basically passive investors who only share in the profits and losses in some proportion to their investment. Limited partners are not personally liable for the debts of the partnership. They have no default right to manage or direct the partnership.

6. Terms of partnerships:

A partnership agreement, if available, may also outline how long the partnership will be in existence. If there is no partnership agreement in place, the partnership will be considered a partnership-at-will.

Partners in a **partnership-at-will** have the right to cause the partnership to end at any time with or without having a cause to do so (subject to certain penalties if there is no lawful cause to do so).

Partners in a **partnership-for-term** agree to be in the partnership together for a specific period of time.

Partners in a **limited-scope-partnership** agree to be in the partnership together until the completion of a specific project. A **joint venture**, though considered a separate method of doing business under many state statutes, is analogized to this type of partnership in most jurisdictions.

7. Sources of Law: UPA & RUPA

The Uniform Partnership Act ("UPA") was created in 1914 and consequently adopted in all states except Louisiana.

The UPA was revised in 1997 to create the Revised Uniform Partnership Act ("RUPA"). RUPA has been adopted in 32 states and is currently under consideration in many others. Because it is in the majority of jurisdictions and represents the most modern understanding of partnership law, the following discussion will cite to RUPA rather than UPA.

RUPA provides guidance for these major areas of partnership law:
- finding whether a partnership exists or not
- defining the relationship between or among all partners
- defining the relationship between each partner and the partnership

Agency & Partnership
SPARK LAW SERIES

- defining the relationship between each partner and a third party
- defining the relationship between the partnership and a third party
- providing guidelines for the ending of a partnership relationship.

Remember that the partnership agreement (a contract) will be the main source for determining the parameters of the partnership relationship, subject to doctrines in contract law such as formation, interpretation of terms, and unconscionability (just as in any other contract). In the absence of contract or in the case of a disputed contract, the model codes discussed below become the main source of guidance for the court.

> RUPA § 103: Effect of Partnership Agreement; Nonwaivable Provisions
> (a) Except as otherwise provided . . . , relations among partners and between the partners and the partnership are governed by the partnership agreement. To the extent the partnership agreement does not otherwise provide, this [Act] governs relations . . .

Additionally, the provisions of RUPA relating mostly to specific partner duties are considered unwaivable by any contract. Examples of duties that you cannot "contract around" are the duty of loyalty and duty of care.

> RUPA § 103: Effect of Partnership Agreement; Nonwaivable Provisions
> (b) The partnership agreement may not:
>
> (3) eliminate the duty of loyalty . . .
> (4) unreasonably reduce the duty of care . . .
> (5) eliminate the obligation of good faith . . .

Agency & Partnership
SPARK LAW SERIES

Defining a Partnership

General Definition

A partnership is a particular kind of business formed when **two or more persons** act as **co-owners** of a business **for profit**, whether or not they intend to form a partnership.

> RUPA § 101 (6): Definitions
> "Partnership" means an association of two or more persons to carry on as co-owners a business for profit formed under [this Act or comparable law].

Example: Larry, Moe, and Curly decide to open a business together. They all contribute money to help get the business started, share the profits that come in, and divide up the work among themselves. They have more than likely formed a partnership even if they never call the business a "partnership."

Characteristics of a Partnership

The hallmark characteristics of a partnership are shared ownership, shared control, and shared liability. Shared ownership is what creates a partnership, shared control is what maintains the partnership, and share liability is what results from the partnership.

These common characteristics are those that, for the most part, a business must display in order to be considered a partnership by a court.

Profit Sharing

The right to share profits in the business is *the* key prerequisite for defining a partnership.
Profits are generally defined as the amount of revenue generated by a business minus the costs of operating that business. The sharing of profits is viewed as the prime motivation for partners to act in the best interests of a partnership. Profit sharing alone is a *necessary factor* to prove that a partnership exists, but is usually *insufficient* on its own.

Agency & Partnership
SPARK LAW SERIES

Loss Sharing

While not usually considered a prerequisite for finding a partnership, the sharing of business losses is very strong evidence pointing to a partnership relationship.

Co-Ownership

Partners usually co-own the assets of the partnership business in that all partners have the right to control the use of such property and also share in the gains and losses of such property.

Co-Management

Though certainly not a necessary characteristic, many partners share in the managing of the partnership business whether on a day-to-day level or on a more removed executive level.

Partnership Distinguished From Other Business Relationships

Partnership vs. Agency: The primary distinction between a partnership and an agency relationship is that a partnership is comprised of partners or co-owners of the business, while an agency relationship is comprised of employers and employees.

Fenwick v. Unemployment Compensation Commission, 133 N.J.L. 295, 44 A. 2d 172 (1945) (partner or employee?)

The question before the court in this case was whether a receptionist and owner of a beauty shop who entered into a "partnership agreement" were actually in a valid partnership.

The court found that *no partnership was formed* even though the parties called themselves partners and shared in the profits. The court analyzed the following factors:

1) 100% of the assets remained with the owner
2) 100% of the control remained with the owner
3) 100% of the loses were borne by the owner

4) There was an 80%/20% split on net profits but in this instance the 20% net profit participation functioned in the place of wages for the receptionist.
5) The receptionist was a prior employee and appeared to third parties to be under the supervision of the owner.

RUPA § 202: Formation of Partnership
(c) A person who receives a portion of the profits in a business is presumed to be a partner unless:
    (i.) the payments are in return for services as an independent contractor or regular wages as an employee

Partnership vs. Joint Venture: A joint venture also features co-owners which agree to share in profits and losses but, unlike a partnership, is formed for the purposes of a *single* business transaction. Because joint ventures resemble partnerships in every other aspect besides the length of engagement, courts often apply the laws of partnership to joint venture situations.

FORMING A PARTNERSHIP

By Contract

An express or implied contract is needed to form a partnership as a partnership is always a voluntary, consensual association of interests. Without consent from all the parties, a partnership cannot be formed.

> A written contract (in the form of a partnership agreement), while not necessary to form a partnership, is usually undeniable evidence of consent.

In the Absence of a Agreed-Upon Contract

If the parties cannot agree that a partnership was formed or the terms of the partnership agreement are in dispute, the law looks at certain factors to determine whether a partnership exists or not.

Agency & Partnership
SPARK LAW SERIES

RUPA § 202: Formation of Partnership
(a) The association of two or more persons to act as co-owners of a business for profit are considered partners, whether or not they intended to form a partnership.

(b) . . .

The key factor, as mentioned above, is sharing of profits. The sharing of profits from a business is usually indisputable evidence that a partnership exists. The rationale is that no other reason for sharing the profits of a business with a person makes sense unless the person is a partner.

Other factors that courts consider:

1) Contribution of Capital: Though not essential, contributing capital to an enterprise is indicative of a partnership agreement.

2) Parties' Own Designation: The mere fact that parties call one another a "partner" can be meaningful but is not conclusive proof of a partnership existing.

Partnership by Estoppel

Estoppel in general is an idea born from equity. A partnership by estoppel may be created in regard to dealings **with a third party** in certain situations. The partnership by estoppel doctrine dictates that when someone pretends to be a partner (or goes along with representations that he or she is partner), she will be liable to any third party who extends credit on reliance of that representation.

Agency & Partnership
SPARK LAW SERIES

FIDUCIARY DUTIES IN PARTNERSHIP

Duty of Loyalty

A partner is bound to be loyal to her partnership specifically with regard to the following areas:

> Duty of Accounting
> A partner must account to the partnership any property, money or other benefit derived by the partner in the conduct of the partnership business or that results from the partnership position.

Meinhard v. Salmon, 249 N.Y. 458, 164 N.E. 545 (1928) (Cardozo) (partners in a lease)

Two partners, Meinhard and Salmon, leased some property together. Right before the lease was to expire, Salmon made a deal with a third party regarding the property but without including Meinhard.

The court held that Salmon had violated the duty of loyalty owed to Meinhard because the new deal was an extension of the old lease (in other words, the new deal covered the business of the partnership) and that Salmon had a duty to *disclose* the opportunity to his partner at a minimum.

> Duty to Not Compete
> A partner cannot engage in conduct that directly competes with the partnership without the consent of all the other partners. If a partner does compete with consent, she must account for all profits derived from the competitive conduct to the partnership.

Meehan v. Shaughnessy, 404 Mass. 419, 535 N.E.2d 1255 (1989) (law partners soliciting clients)

The partners in a law firm decided to leave and solicited other employees to follow them. They also sent letters to clients explaining why the clients should switch to the new firm.

The court held that soliciting clients for the new firm was a breach of the partners' fiduciary duty because the letter gave the new firm an unfair

Agency & Partnership
SPARK LAW SERIES

advantage. The partnership agreement contemplated that partners may leave and take clients with them, but the current firm must be given an opportunity to compete for such clients. The court ignores the issue of taking away other employees. Cf. **Bancroft-Whitney**.

Duty of Exclusivity

If a partner has promised to devote her services to the partnership on a full-time basis, she may not render services to any other employer without the consent of all the other partners. In doing so, even with consent, any wages derived from such conduct would be considered partnership income.

Bane v. Ferguson, 890 F.2d 11 (7th Cir. 1989) (Posner) (retired law partner with no more retirement benefits)

The plaintiff was a former partner of a law firm. He lost his retirement benefits after a disastrous merger and bad management practices caused the firm to dissolve. Plaintiff alleged a violation of fiduciary duties.

The Court held that no fiduciary duties exist between current and former partners because a former partner has, by definition, left the partnership.

Duty of Care

Each partner has a duty to refrain from gross negligence, recklessness, intentional misconduct and knowingly unlawful conduct while working on behalf of the partnership.

Agency & Partnership
SPARK LAW SERIES

RIGHTS OF PARTNERS IN MANAGEMENT & AUTHORITY TO BIND

Shared Management

In most small partnerships, each partner expects and is expected to play a role in conducting the business of the partnership. The right of each partner to participate in the business' operations is implicit to the partnership agreement.

> RUPA § 401: Partners' Rights and Duties
> (f) Each partner has equal rights in the management and conduct of the partnership business.

Yet, disagreements inevitably arise about business decisions. In the absence of an agreement to the contrary, the default rule is that all partners have equal rights to the management of the business. Decisions about ordinary matters are to be decided by a majority of the partners. Decisions about larger matters which involve the heart of the business must be agreed to unanimously by all the partners.

National Biscuit Company v. Stroud, 249 N.C. 467, 106 S.E.2d 692 (1959) (buying bread without permission)

Both partners in a two person partnership disagreed about the purchase of bread. One partner bought bread without consent from the other partner. Buying bread was an everyday decision but majority rule is unavailable in a 2-person situation.

The court finds that each partner has the power to enter into binding contracts as long as the conduct is part of the 1) normal course of business and 2) does not harm the other partner.

Binding the Partnership in Contract

Every partner is an agent of the partnership for purposes of the partnership business. Therefore, any contract that a partner enters into for the purposes of carrying on the normal business of the partnership binds the entire partnership, unless the partner really had no such authority and the third party knew that the partner lacked such authority.

Agency & Partnership
SPARK LAW SERIES

RUPA § 301: Partner Agent of Partnership
(1) . . . An act of a partner, including the execution of an instrument in the partnership name, for apparently carrying on in the ordinary course the partnership business or business of the kind carried on by the partnership binds the partnership, unless the partner had no authority to act for the partnership in the particular matter and the person with whom the partner was dealing knew or had received notification that the partner lacked authority.

Binding the Partnership in Tort

Partners are jointly and severally liable for torts that injure third parties. Because of this joint and several liability, an action may be brought against any single partner without naming all the other partners.

RUPA § 305: Partnership Liabile for Partner's Actionable Conduct
(a) A partnership is liable for loss or injury caused to a person . . . as a result of a wrongful act or omission, or other actionable conduct, of a partner acting in the ordinary course of business of the partnership or with authority of the partnership.

RUPA § 306: Partner's Liability
(1) Except [for obligations incurred before a partner joins the partnership or in the case of LLPs], all partners are liable jointly and severally for all obligations of the partnership unless otherwise agreed by the claimant or provided by law.

Agency & Partnership
SPARK LAW SERIES

ENDING A PARTNERSHIP: IN GENERAL

The end of any relationship is messy, and partnerships are no different. There are three main concepts with regard to the ending of a partnership.

Dissociation is where a partner no longer wishes to be part of a partnership. Every partner has the power to dissociate at any time but, unless specifically provided, leaving the partnership will be considered wrongful. A wrongful dissociation will have certain financial consequences for a partner.

Dissolution is merely the beginning to ending the partnership. Once a partnership is in dissolution, it is recognized that it is no longer in business except to finish up projects already started and to settle accounts among all the partners.

Winding up is the actual finishing of the partnership business and the settlement of accounts among the partners. Dissolution is the precursor to winding up. Once a partnership (in dissolution) finishes winding up, it is then no longer in existence.

> *RUPA § 802: Partnership Continues After Dissolution*
> *. . . a partnership continues after dissolution only for the purpose of winding up its business. The partnership is terminated when the winding up of its business is completed.*

Agency & Partnership
SPARK LAW SERIES

ENDING A PARTNERSHIP: DISSOCIATION

Disagreements, changed circumstances, bad business, and a host of other reasons may lead a partner or several partners to no longer wish to be part of the partnership.

A partner can dissociate from the partnership either voluntarily or not. Every partner has the power to dissociate at any time, though not necessarily the right to do so. A partnership can remain in existence after a partner dissociates (voluntarily) or is dissociated (involuntarily). The other option is for the entire partnership to dissolve in which case the partnership will then only be in the business of "winding up."

Events Causing Dissociation

Dissociation means that the individual will no longer be considered a partner of the business. The dissociation of a partner from a partnership can occur in five main ways:

(1) Express Will

The partner expressly wishes to withdraw from the partnership and does so. The effect of a partner expressly dissociating from the partnership is for the partnership to enter into dissolution.

If the partnership agreement is at-will, then a partner may leave the partnership at any time without violating the agreement.

(2) Partnership Agreement

Some partnership agreements condition the length of a partner's involvement with the business on the basis of the occurrence of an agreed-upon event. Once that event occurs, the partner is dissociated.

(3) Expulsion

Agency & Partnership
SPARK LAW SERIES

Expulsion procedures are usually outlined in the partnership agreement. If there is no violation of those agreed-upon expulsion terms, then the dissociation of a partner by expulsion does not violate the partnership agreement.

(4) Unanimous Vote

If all partners unanimously agree to do so, a partner may be dissociated in this fashion.

(5) Judicial Dissociation

A court of law can effect the dissociation of partner from a partnership if the partner engages in:

(a) wrongful conduct that hurts the partnership
(b) willful or persistent breach of the partnership agreement or duties owed to other partners

(c) behavior which makes it not reasonably practicable to carry on business with that partner

Power to Dissociate

Each partner has the power to leave the partnership at any time.

This dissociation will be deemed wrongful, though, if:

(1) it breaches the partnership agreement
(2) in the case of a term or specific-project partnership, the partner leaves before completion of the term

    a. There is an exception if a partner dissociates within 90 days after the dissociation of another partner.

Consequences of Dissociation

To the Former Partner:
In the case of a wrongful dissociation, the former partner is liable to the partnership for any damages caused by his dissociation. The former partner's right to participate in management and his duty of loyalty ends.

Agency & Partnership
SPARK LAW SERIES

A duty of loyalty and care only continues as to matters which arose before the dissociation.

The interest of the former partner is then subject to being bought out by the other partners.

To the Partnership:
The remaining partners can choose to continue or dissolve the partnership.

If the partnership continues, the remaining partners can seize the capital of the wrongful former partner and use it for the partnership. The former partner can collect on the interest gained on that seized capital but not immediately, and the interest will always be fair market value even if the partnership becomes incredibly profitable after his departure.

If the partnership decides to dissolve, the remaining money held by the partnership is distributed among each remaining partner.

Agency & Partnership
SPARK LAW SERIES

ENDING A PARTNERSHIP: DISSOLUTION

Events Causing Dissolution

A partnership **can** only be dissolved upon occurrence of:

(1) a partner's express will to dissociate from the partnership

(2) term partnership conditioned to end upon the occurrence of a specific event

(3) a particular event agreed upon in the partnership agreement

(4) judicial dissolution determined when:

> (i) the economic purpose of the partnership is unreasonably frustrated
>
> (ii) another partner has engaged in conduct related to the partnership which makes it unreasonable to continue a partnership with that person
>
> (iii) no longer practicable to carry on the partnership business in accordance with the partnership agreement.

Judicial Dissolution

Judicial dissolution is easier to procure than judicial dissociation because the life of the entire partnership is ending, so there is less scrutiny. Judicial dissolution results in less remedies as well.

The standard for declaring a judicial dissolution is that 1) it is not reasonably practicable to continue the partnership, or 2) the economic purpose of the partnership has been unreasonably frustrated.

Agency & Partnership
SPARK LAW SERIES

Owen v. Cohen, 19 Cal. 2d 147, 119 P. 2d 713 (1941) (bowling alley partnership)

Plaintiff sought a judicial dissolution of the partnership because the parties disagreed on practically all matters essential to operation of the partnership business.

Court found for judicial dissolution using the following three element standard:

(1) partner is guilty of conduct that hurts the business

(2) partner willfully or persistently breaches the partnership agreement or otherwise conducts himself in a way so that it is not reasonably practicable to carry on a partnership

(3) other equitable circumstances.

Agency & Partnership
SPARK LAW SERIES

QUESTIONS & ANSWERS

PROBLEM 1.1: *The Firm and its Agents and Servants*

While swimming behind a boat in Peaceful Valley Lake in Missouri, Bunting died of acute carbon monoxide poisoning. Mercury Marine, Inc manufactured the boat's motor. Under Missouri law, Mercury Marine may be sued either in the county in which the accident happened, or in any other county in which it "keeps an office or agent for the transaction of its usual and customary business." Mercury Marine has no office in St. Louis, but Dealer sells its boat motors in that city. Mercury Marine appointed Dealer as its "authorized dealer for the retail sale, display, and servicing" of its products. Under the agreement between them:
(a) Mercury Marine sells its products to Dealer for resale. Dealer is free to sell products made by other manufacturers.
(b) Dealer gives Mercury Marine's warranty to all buyers of Mercury Marine products.
(c) Dealer performs warranty svc on Mercury Marine products. Mercury Marine honors warranty claims "made by purchaser through Dealer" and reimburses Dealer for warranty svc it performs "on behalf of Mercury Marine."

a. <u>Is Dealer Mercury Marine's agent for purposes of determining venue?</u> (*see State* ex. rel. *Bunting v. Koehr*, 865 SW2d 351 (Mo. 1993)

<u>Answer:</u>

The TEST for determining whether an "agency" existed is three-pronged: YOU NEED ALL OF THEM TO SATISFY THE AGENCY RELATIONSHIP; in order for agent/principle relationship to exist here A would have to only exclusively sell those goods and not any other goods (From Green v. HR Block). For example: If dealer buys the good and gets title such as best buy's computers and then resells this is not a PA relationship but merely a buyer seller relationship. If you work at Gateway and only sell the certain products and don't get title this will be PA relationship. REMEMBER: if close cases the courts will find an agency relationship to not deter commerce.

Agency & Partnership
SPARK LAW SERIES

(1) "Agent" must hold a power to alter legal relations between the principal and 3rd persons and between the principal and himself. (if element one is satisfied then 3 is clearly satisfied since if you have the power to alter legal relationship between P and third party then he obviously has the power to control conduct of the agent).
    a. The warranty here was specific in the warranty and the dealer cannot alter it, therefore they cannot change the warranty. Because the K is very specific the dealer is not able to alter the legal relationship so that would elude us to fact that there is not an agent relationship here.

(2) The agent is a fiduciary with respect to matters within the scope of his agency.
    a. Res 2nd 13 (pg 165 Supp)

(3) The principal has the right to control the conduct of the agent w/ respect to matters entrusted to him.
    a. Res 2nd 14 (pg 165 supplement)

§ Agency; Principle; Agent
(1) Agency is the fiduciary relation which results from the manifestation of consent by one person (P) to another (A) that the other (A) shall act on his (P) behalf and subject to his (P) control, and consent by the other so (A) to act.
(2) The one for whom action is to be taken is the principle.
(3) The one who is to act is the agent.

The absence of ANY one of these three elements of agency defeats a claim that agency exists. HERE, the dealer does not sell Mercury Marine products principally for the benefit of Mercury Marine. The Dealer is independent of Mercury Marine, is permitted to sell products of competing companies, and purchases Mercury Marine motors primarily for the purpose of reselling them for its own profit. The relationship between the dealers and Mercury Marine for the sale of Mercury Marine products is, THEREFORE, that of buyer and seller, NOT agent and principal. THE BUYER SELLER RELATIONSHIP ALONE WOULD NOT CREATE AN AGENCY RELATIONSHIP!! (See class notes pg 16).

Agency & Partnership
SPARK LAW SERIES

b. <u>Is the fact that Dealer extended and perfected Mercury Marine's product warranty for the ultimate purchaser sufficient factual predicate to support the legal conclusion that Dealer is Mercury Marine's agent</u>?

   ANSWER:

   Agency does not exist unless the dealer has the "power to alter the legal relationship" between Mercury Marine and the ultimate purchaser." HERE, the dealer agrees to extend the warranty to any subsequent purchaser of the motor and notify Mercury Marine of the new holder of the warranty. This contractual obligation is NOT the same as a power to alter a legal relationship between the manufacturer and the purchaser. WHY? B/c the manufacturer
   (1) <u>Sells</u> the product to the dealer for resale;
   (2) <u>Unilaterally</u> imposes the terms of the warranty prior to the sale to the dealer;
   (3) Forbids the dealer from altering the terms of the warranty in any way;
   (4) Requires the dealer to extend the warranty as part of the sale and notify the manufacturer of the new holder of the warranty; AND
   (5) Makes the warranty a part of the purchaser's bargain when he or she purchases the product.
   UNDER THESE CIRCUMSTANCES, there is no agency between the manufacturer and the dealer as there is no power in the dealer to alter the legal relationship between the manufacturer and the purchaser.

c. <u>Does Dealer's obligation to provide warranty svc make it Mercury Marine's agent</u>?

   ANSWER:

   NO. Although "control" over the dealers' warranty work is a necessary element of agency, it nevertheless does not exist UNLESS both of the remaining elements of agency are also present. The dealer's obligation to perform warranty work is NOT tantamount to a power to alter Mercury Marine's legal relationship w/ a third party. Even here when you kick in control you are not satisfying the first prong from above.

PROBLEM 1.2: The Firm and its Agents and Servants
(Same as Problem 4.3 – see below)

ABC Corp. sold mobile homes and developed mobile home parks. ABC employed Agent, a licensed real estate broker, to acquire land for development as mobile home parks, at a weekly salary of $125. Agent told ABC that Parkacre was available for purchase. ABC asked Agent to purchase the land as a "straw man," and then to convey the land to ABC. Agent told ABC that the land would cost $30,000, and ABC gave Agent that amount.

Unknown to ABC, Agent had an interest in Parkacre. Before he had been employed by ABC, Agent had paid $1,000 for an option to buy Parkacre for $15,000. When ABC gave Agent the $30,000 he asked for, Agent exercised his option to buy Parkacre. Agent then used $14,000 of the $30,000 to complete the purchase, and kept the remaining $16,000.

ABC has now sued Agent for breach of fiduciary duty, asking that Agent be required to give ABC the entire $15,000 profit on the transaction. Agent argues that ABC's sole remedy is to rescind the transaction – return Parkacre in exchange for the $30,000 purchase price.

<u>Answer:</u>

The <u>Fiduciary Principle</u> entails that an agreement to act on behalf of the principal causes the agent to have a DUTY imposed on him, created by his undertaking, <u>to act primarily for the benefit of another in matters connected with his undertaking</u>. Among the duties to the principal are:
    a. the duty to account for profits arising out of the employment,
    b. the duty not to act as, or on account of, an adverse party without the principal's consent,

Agency & Partnership
SPARK LAW SERIES

    c. the duty not to compete w/ the principal on his own account or for another in matters relating to the subject matter of the agency, AND

    d. the duty to deal fairly w/ the principal in all transactions between them.

<u>Restatement §387</u> states that an agent's duty as a fiduciary requires the agent "to act SOLELY for the benefit of the principal in all matters connected w/ the agency." (one cannot serve two masters, including oneself)

<u>Restatement §389</u> An agent must give profits of a transaction to the principal unless there is an agreement.

<u>Restatement §389</u> An agent is subject to a duty not to deal w/ his principal as an adverse party in a transaction connected w/ the agency <u>w/o the principal's knowledge</u>.

<u>Restatement §390</u> An agent who, <u>with the knowledge of the principal</u>, acts on his own account in a transaction in which he is employed has a duty of deal fairly and disclose everything to the principal unless the principle manifest that he knows the facts or does not care. (so even if the agent disclosed the option, he still had a duty to deal fairly)

<u>Restatement §403</u> states that where "an agent receives anything as a result of his violation of a duty of loyalty to the principal, he is subject to a liability <u>to deliver it, its value, or its proceeds, to the principal</u>." (The traditional *equitable remedy* is the Constructive Trust.)

NOTE: Remember Judge Cardozo (in *Meinhard v. Salmon*) – "Not honesty alone but the punctilio of an honor most sensitive is the standard of behavior."

<u>Remedies that Principal has</u>:
- Get all the profits that are derived from the relationship (especially secret ones).
- Constructive Trust w/ agent as trustee: court implies one.
- Get the value of the use of his property.

Agency & Partnership
SPARK LAW SERIES

PROBLEM 2.1: *Firm's Liability in Contract for Acts of its Agents*

Equipment owner Kapperman was negotiating the possible sale of his broken road grader to Schladweiler for about $8500. Kapperman authorized Schladweiler only to obtain three bids to have the engine repair work done (so that Kapperman could then decide whether the repair was affordable). Instead, Schladweiler represented to Truck Repair that he had authority from Kapperman to obtain the repair on behalf of Kapperman, as long as the cost of the repair did not exceed $3500. Schladweiler did not get any other bids and ordered the work done by Truck Repair. Truck Repair did the work for $6400, released the road grader to Schladweiler, but has not been paid. Schladweiler is insolvent. Who is liable for the repair bill?

ANSWER:

The principle is only liable if there is actual or apparent authority. (R)

The Principal is not liable at all – since there was no authority. P gave actual authority to give bids only. P did not authorize the work done, he just authorized him to get bids. But here in this situation A is liable for the whole amount.

Caveat: if he was authorized for repait then P would only be authorized for the exact amount. P expressly authorized (Actual authority: see 7 below) to spend 3.5k. Therefore, since the agent went above that he would be liable for the rest.

Restatement §7 – Authority is defined as the power of the agent to affect the legal relations of the principal by acts done in accordance with the principal's manifestations of consent to him. **(Here there were no such manifestations)**

Restatement §164(1) – Where an agent enters into an unauthorized contract w/o having the power to bind the principal, the principal is NOT bound by the contract as actually made by the agent, or as it would have been made if the agent had acted w/in his or her authority. Since A was given actual authority as to amount he is liable for that amount.

Restatement §§8, 8A, and 8B – However, under certain circumstances agents may have power to bind the principal by unauthorized acts, such as where the agent has apparent authority or inherent agency power, or where the principal is estopped (b/c a 3rd party relied) from denying the agent's authority. (None of which are present in this case) (see page 164 supplement)

The Principal must have the capacity to give legal consent, as well as capacity to do the act that he or she is authorizing his agent to do.

The Agent, however, must only have the physical or mental capability to do the act (not legal). Therefore, a minor can act as an agent AND can bind a principal to a contract.

PROBLEM 2.2: Undisclosed Principals

Acton was in business in Chicago as a retailer dealer in costume jewelry. I addition, he frequently served as a purchasing agent for retailer of similar goods. In December, Pace, a retailer for whom Acton had occasionally acted in the past, wrote Acton authorizing him to purchase on Pace's behalf a specified quantity of costume jewelry form Tab, a wholesaler. Pace added that b/c of certain transactions in the past, Tab might refuse to deal with him and directed Acton not to disclose the buyer's identity. Acton, who occasionally dealt with Tab on his own account, was indebted to Tab for $3500 for various items purchased on credit earlier that year under contracts that were reasonable and provident when made. Acton immediately contacted Tab and arranged with him for the purchase of the costume jewelry. A written contract was entered into, delivery to be made Feb. 1 at Acton's place of business, payment to be made 10 days thereafter. Acton signed the contract in his own name, having made no mention of Pace, and Tab assumed that Acton was the buyer. On Feb 1, Tab failed to deliver under the contract, notifying Acton that he had learned for whom Acton was acting and that he would not fill the order. Informed of this, Pace promptly purchased similar costume

Agency & Partnership
SPARK LAW SERIES

jewelry in the open market. Pace suffered damages of $3500 with respect to the costume jewelry. Pave demanded that Tab pay him $3500 damages. Tab repeated his refusal to be bound by the contract, pointing out that had Tab known the identity of Acton's principal, he would not have entered into the contract. Tab also claimed that even if he were liable, he would be entitled to set off the $3500 owed him by Acton. What are Pace's rights, if any, against Tab? Give Reasons.

ANSWER:

Pace: P. Acton A, Tab: 3rd party
If P sues T: then T is not L since P was undisclosed (303), but under 302 T would be liable unless 3 exceptions are met (however 302 is not met since the second of prong of fraud was met here).
If T sues A: A is liable (306)
If T sues P:

1. Ordinarily an <u>agent</u> is not liable for a <u>disclosed</u> principal, <u>but if the principal is undisclosed</u> then agent *is* on the hook. It is as though the agent is the only one involve until the principal is disclosure. The agent is completely off the hook post-disclosure.
2. If principal contracts with the agent to keep disclosure, unwarranted disclosure does not preclude the ability of the 3rd to sue the principal.
3. Agents continued exposure – any trust or confidence in the agent will bind the agent. So you cannot shift responsibility to the principal if the 3rd party was relying on the ability of the agent. The 3rd party has remedy here against the agent. The remedy here might be that
4. <u>Restatement §4</u> – Disclosed Principal; Partially Disclosed Principal; Undisclosed Principal – if the other party has no notice that the agent is acting for a principal then the on for whom he acts is undisclosed.
5. <u>Common Law</u> – an undisclosed principal is bound by the acts of the agent, Accordingly, they can also sue 3rd parties (since they are on the hook)
6. <u>Restatement §302</u> – 3rd parties are bound to the undisclosed principal unless (3 exceptions):
    i. The agreement states to the contrary
    ii. Existence of principal is <u>fraudulently concealed</u>

Agency & Partnership
SPARK LAW SERIES

          iii. There is a set off or similar defense against the agent.
7. See also Restatement §303, §304
     i. 303: A person (3rd party) with whom an agent makes a contract on account of an undisclosed principle is not liable in an action at law brought upon the contract by such principle:
          i. If the contract is in the form of a sealed or negotiation instrument OR
          ii. If the terms of the contract exclude liability to any undisclosed principle or to the particularly principle.
    (4) 306(1) : The principle is on the hook unless limits exposure. One the agent is liable he can't throw it onto the principle and the A would be liable. However here, Tab found out who the principle was so therefore this section drops out of the analysis.

PROBLEM 3.1: Contracts Entered into before LLC Formation

Grace and Alice were starting their own record label, "White Rabbit Records." Grace's father, Lewis, agreed to invest in the business. The three of them agreed to organize the business as a limited liability company, in which Grace, Alice and Lewis were to be the only members.

Lewis gave Grace and Alice $100,000, which they deposited in a bank account under the name "White Rabbit Records." Grace started looking for a place to put the recording studio and offices. Alice started working on finding recording artists. On March 7, Alice signed a recording contract w/ Artist. The recording contract was in the name of "White Rabbit Records," and was signed as follows:
                      White Rabbit Records
                      By: */S/ Alice*

Using forms she downloaded from the Internet, Grace prepared Articles of Organization for a limited liability company to be named "Whit Rabbit Records, LLC." On April 1, the three signed the Articles of Organization, and mailed them to Secretary of State of the State of

Agency & Partnership
SPARK LAW SERIES

Confusion for filing under the Confusion Limited Liability Co Act ("CLLCA").

Lewis invested in the business, but was not active in its operation. Grace and Alice both invested in, and were active in running the business. While Alice was off contacting bands and songwriters, Grace found a place to put their recording studio. On April 7, Grace signed a lease w/ Landlord. The lease showed "White Rabbit Records, LLC" as the lessee, and was signed as follows:

White Rabbit Records
By: <u>/S/ Grace</u>
Grace, member

On April 15, Grace received a letter from the Confusion Secretary of State, returning the Articles of Organization of White Rabbit Records, LLC, and advising that the Articles were being returned **without filing**, b/c the name "White Rabbit Records, LLC" was not available w/o a letter of consent from White Rabbit Magic, Inc. Grace, Alice and Lewis obtained the letter of consent, and mailed the consent, and the Articles of Organization for White Rabbit Records, LLC, to the Confusion Secretary of State. The Confusion Secretary of State accepted the Articles of Organization for filing, and issued a Certificate of Organization for White Rabbit Records, LLC, effective as of April 22.

Questions:
  (1) Please advise each of Grace, Alice, Lewis and White Rabbit Records, LLC as to their respective responsibilities w/ respect to
      (a) the recording contract w/ Artist, and
      (b) the lease w/ Landlord. You may assume that, except as set forth above, the Lease has no provisions that would affect your answer.
  (2) Suppose that, instead of a limited liability company, the parties had formed a limited partnership, w/ Grace and Alice as general partners, and Lewis as a limited partner. Would that change the responsibilities of the parties on the Lease? Why or why not?

Agency & Partnership
SPARK LAW SERIES

ANSWER:

(1) Advice to Grace, Alice, and Lewis as to their responsibilities w/ respect to:

   (a) <u>The Recording Contract w/ Artist</u> –

      Alice acted as a promoter of the corporate enterprise, White Rabbit Records, LLC, when she signed the recording contract. The legal relationship between a promoter and a not-yet formed entity is analogous to that of agent/principal. As such, promoters are at least initially liable on any contracts they execute in furtherance of the corporate entity prior to its formation. The promoters are released from liability <u>only when:</u>

        (i)   The contract provides that performance is to be the obligation of the corporation (novation)
        (ii)   The corporation is ultimately formed (de jeure)
        (iii) The corporation then formally adopts the contract (ratification and affirmation).

      Pre-incorporation agreements merely indicate that it is undertaken on behalf of a corporation and the corp will not be exclusively liable in the event of a breach – the promoter remains liable on the contract.

Promoter Liability – The promoter will only be released from liability IF:

        (i)   The corp is ultimately formed AND
        (ii)   the corp subsequently <u>ADOPTS</u> the contract and
        (iii) there is subsequent <u>NOVATION</u>. However, in order for the liability to shift to the later-formed corp, the contract must explicitly state that the performance thereunder is solely the responsibility of the corp.

THEREFORE, *Alice* will be held liable to Artist unless White Rabbit Records, LLC adopts the contract. Upon novation of the contract, liability will shift from Alice to the corp. White Rabbit Records is not liable because it does not exist. Artist can look only to Alice for liability (e is an argument that Grace could be liable as a general partner under default rules but probably not Lewis because he has no control. Lewis probably falls under §304(a). If Artist looks to corp/entity for liability they will be estopped from doing so since they knew that the entity wasn't formed the artist cant sue the entity.

Agency & Partnership
SPARK LAW SERIES

You can argue that Alice is an agent of an undisclosed principle (entity) and therefore 320, 321, and 322 might be applicable. Since Alice (A) was disclosed we would apply 321 and 322. But it would really be more 321 (they knew there was a record company but not the name (pg 182 supp).

304a Analysis: see pg 340 in supplement (Alice and Grace: GPs and Lewis LP)

(b) <u>The Lease w/ Landlord</u>
    Grace, like Alice, acted as a promoter to the corp/partnership entity when she signed the lease.

    <u>Restatement §326</u> – There is an inference that a person intends to make a present contract w/ an existing person. If, therefore, both parties know that there is no principal capable of entering into such a contract, there is a rebuttable inference that, although the contract is nominally in the name of the nonexistent person, the parties intend that the person signing as agent should be a party, unless there is some indication to the contrary. (see pg 182 supp).
    <u>LLC Liability</u> – The LLC will not be liable UNLESS:
    (i)   The contract provides that performance is solely the responsibility of the corporation.
    (ii)   If it doesn't, then the LLC must make an affirmative act that shows that it has ADOPTED the contract after formation. There are two ways in which an entity can ADOPT a contract:
        (A) Expressly, or
        (B) By Conduct (accepting the benefits and fruits of the contract) – like RATIFICATION.

    The key in advising Grace and Alice is to tell them to have an express provision in the contract that states that the LLC is assuming sole liability and responsibility and that they are merely acting as agents for the LLC. Ultimately, Grace is bound personally by the lease she signed with the landlord. Under a LLP both Grace and Alice are liable for the lease. There may be some estoppel argument if there was reliance.

(2) If partners had formed as a Limited Partnership –

Agency & Partnership
SPARK LAW SERIES

Yes the formation of a limited partnership would change the responsibilities of the parties on the lease that Grace signed. The parties would be held to different standards of liability on the Lease. In order to have an LP, certain steps need to be taken and as long as there is substantial compliance with the statute, the LP will be recognized. However, if there has been no compliance yet, the default rule is to take it as a general partnership. As such, both Alice and Grace will be held liable as general partners on the Lease. The general partnership default rules are found RUPA §202.

On the Lease, Lewis would be held to a different standard and he would probably win under the next section:

<u>ULPA §304</u> (P.340)– A person who makes a contribution to a business enterprise and erroneously but in good faith believes that he has become a limited partner in the enterprise is not a general partner in the enterprise and is not bound by its obligations by reason of making the contribution, receiving distribution from the enterprise, or exercising any rights of a ltd partner, if, on ascertaining the mistake, he or she:
- o Causes an appropriate certificate of limited partnership or a certificate of amendment to be executed and filed; or
- o Withdraws from future equity participation in the enterprise by executing and filing in the office of the Sec of State a certificate declaring withdrawal under this section.

Artist, however, could argue that since no attempt had even been made yet as to filing the Articles of Organization, that it should be a general partnership rendering Lewis personally liable too. The <u>general rule</u> is that 3rd party's knowledge regarding the status of a ltd partnership is irrelevant when at the time of contracting, the partners have made no attempt to comply w/ the filing requirements. Since they were de facto (meaning they made a good faith colorable attempt to comply with the statutory requirements) they would not be de jeure and therefore not an LLC. Then the default rules for GP would apply. If now they were GPs, Alice and Grace would be liable since they, under 304, actively participated. Lewis could then argue under 304b that since he was passive he would not be liable (since a LP in a GP)

Agency & Partnership
SPARK LAW SERIES

Lewis could then argue that b/c he had no active control or participation in the company he is a limited partner and as such, not liable. The rebuttal, however, by Artist would be the opposite – since he shared in the profits he should be personally liable. AND Artist might win b/c of the non-compliance w/ the filing requirements.

IF an LLC had in fact been formed properly, by definition of an LLC each member has actual authority to bind the LLC. If a member does not agree that member may withdraw or mediate. Since Lewis did neither, he would therefore become liable under the K that bound the LLC. (pg 137 supplement)

Def:
  (1) De facto: (1) There is a statute permitting incorporation, (2) bonafide attempt to incorporate, (3) actual use or attempted use of corp powers (4) third party reliance on the corp.
     i. Result: if you deal with de facto the corporation can be bound by acts of its agents (320 pg 182); disclosed agents and shareholders are not L- L would be imputed to corp.
  (2) De jeure: a matter of strict compliance with statutory requirements
  (3) Corporation by estoppel: when parties are estopped from denying corp.'s existence.

PROBLEM 3.2: Formation of Firms

<u>Contracts Entered into before Formation of a Limited Liability Firm / Interaction of Statutes and Common Law</u>

Investor invested money in Widgets, Ltd. At the time of the investment, Investor signed a Certificate and Agreement of Limited Partnership that specified that Investor would be a limited partner in Widgets, Ltd. Unknown to Investor, Widgets, Ltd. Began doing business without filing the Certificate. After six months, Widgets, Ltd. Distributed $1,000 in profits to Investor. After Investor received the

Agency & Partnership
SPARK LAW SERIES

profits distribution, Investor learned that Widgets, Ltd. was not a limited partnership.

Despite learning that Widgets, Ltd. was not a limited partnership, Investor took no action to procure the filing of the Certificate of Limited partnership for Widgets, Ltd., nor did Investor withdraw from equity participation in the business. In fact, Investor continued to take distributions of profits after Investor learned the business was not a limited partnership.

Widgets, Ltd. is now insolvent, and two of its creditors have sued Investor, seeking to hold Investor personally liable for Widgets, Ltd.'s debts. Alan sold on open account goods worth $10,000 to Widgets, Ltd. after Investor had received the first distribution of profits, but before Investor learned there was no limited partnership. Betty loaned Widgets, Ltd. $25,000, after Investor had learned there was no limited partnership, and after Investor had received further distributions of profits.

Assume that neither Alan nor Betty knew of Investor's involvement with Widgets. Ltd. Under the ULPA, is Investor liable to either Alan or Betty? Under the RULPA?

ANSWER:

The issue is whether Investor in a limited partnership believing to be a limited partner is liable to Alan or Betty for debts owed by Widget. Two rules can answer this question: ULPA §11 and RULPA §304

RULPA §304(a) [see (b) below]: "Person Erroneously Believing Himself Limited Partner. "A person who makes a contribution to a business enterprise and erroneously but in good faith believes that he has become a limited partner in the enterprise is not a general partner in the enterprise and is not bound by its obligations by reason of making the contribution, receiving distributions from the enterprise or exercising any rights of a limited partner, IF, on ascertaining the mistake, HE/SHE:

Agency & Partnership
SPARK LAW SERIES

    (i)   *causes an appropriate certificate of limited partnership or a certificate of amendment to be filed;* OR

    (ii)   *withdraws from future equity participation...by declaring withdraw with the sec of state".*

Applying §304 to the facts presented, Investor made contributions to Widget erroneously, but in good faith he believed that he was a limited partner. He should not be liable to Alan. Alan's sale of 10lk worth of product to Widget (even after Investor receipt of profits) was accomplished *before* Investor learned there was no limited partnership. Conversely, under §304, Investor may be liable to Betty because Investor knew that there was no limited partnership (which is an act of bad faith) when Betty lent the money to Widgets. But Investor might not be liable to Betty (3rd party) because she may have extended the credit without believing in good faith that Investor was a general partner. The applicable section §304(b) reads, "But in either case, only if the third party actually believed in good faith that the person was a general partner at the time of the transaction". Betty has a pretty strong reliance argument, that is, that the credit was extended in good faith. After he found out that they were not a limited partnership (he would now be a GP)

Under ULPA §11: investors in a defective limited partnership will not be treated as general partners so long as (I) they exercised only the rights of limited partners and (ii) they renounce all interest in the business "promptly" on learning that no limited partnership exists. there are no facts indicating that Investor exercised rights beyond his limited partnership but Investor did not renounce interest in the business upon learning that there was no limited partnership because he continued to take distributions of profits after he knew there was no limited partnership. In other words, Investor would be liable as a general partner to Betty not Alan. Not to Alan, because he did not know at the time Investor received distribution that there was no limited partnership, however Investor knew of this at the time Betty lent money to Widget, Ltd. ULPA reasons that because

Agency & Partnership
SPARK LAW SERIES

persons in such a position never actively participate din the control of the business; they were not co-owners of the business, but rather only investors. Therefore as investors, they could involve section 11 and retain any profits received before they learned they were not limited partners. *[This is not bolded because he said only answer with respect to RUPLA.]*

PROBLEM 4.1: Express Actual Authority

You are an associate in a law firm. Your supervising partner assigns you two client files.

A. Leslie Owner owns a small printing shop. Owner is married, and has two young children. Owner is also a member of the National Guard. Owner's unit has just been called into active duty, and is being assigned to Bosnia as a part of the UN peacekeeping forces. Owner wants to execute a general power-of-attorney giving her husband the power to run the printing shop while she is in Bosnia. She also wants her husband to manage her investments, which are her separate property.

B. Grandpa Jones is retired, and has substantial assets that greatly exceed the current exemptions for the imposition of estate taxes. Grandpa is 80 yrs old, and has just been diagnosed w/ Parkinson's disease. Grandpa is too preoccupied w/ his health to pay proper attention to his assets. He also knows that, with his advanced age, and his Parkinson's, it is likely that, in the next year or so, he will become unable to manage his affairs. To ensure that his property will be managed properly, Grandpa wishes to give his daughter a general power-of-attorney.

What should be you concerns in drafting the powers-of-attorney? Are the concerns in drafting Owner's power-of-attorney different from those in drafting Grandpa's? Would further info be helpful in drafting the powers-of-attorney? If you think it would, what info would you like, and why?

Agency & Partnership
SPARK LAW SERIES

ANSWER:

(1) The general rule is that Powers of Attorney are "strictly construed and are held to grant only those powers which are clearly delineated. However, this rule of strict construction is subject to a more important rule: that the court must determine the intention of the parties.

(2) Another accepted rule is to discount or disregard, as meaningless verbiage, all-embracing expressions found in POAs.

(3) Ambiguities are to be resolved against the party who made it or cause it to be made, b/c that party had the better opportunity to understand and explain his meaning.

(4) Finally, general words used in an instrument are restricted by the context in which they are used, and are construed accordingly. Terms are given technical and not popular definitions.

   (a) For Leslie Owner, language such as "such power as may be used in the ordinary course of business" is boilerplate and will probably suffice except if there are unforeseen circumstances. For example, the right to sell, declare bankruptcy, merger, etc. would not be covered in boilerplate language. These things would likely need specific consent.

   (b) For Grandpa there are other issues. Such as continuation on life support and disabilities. For those decisions you would want to get the family's consent ahead of time. Another concern might be Grandpa's competency. Important information, the existence of a will.

   Other powers (*e.g.* power to make gifts of the principal's prop) are NOT included <u>UNLESS</u>
   a. it is expressly conferred
   b. it arises as a <u>necessary implication</u> from the conferred powers, OR
   c. it is <u>clearly intended</u> by the parties, as evidenced by the surrounding facts and circumstances.

2. Guardians of incompetents
   a. Do not have authority to maintain an action for divorce of grandfather absent explicit statutory authorization due to personal nature of the relationship.

Agency & Partnership
SPARK LAW SERIES

The issue then arises, whether the husband has the power to hire someone to manage the printing store. (*See* PROBLEM 4.2 – Implied Actual Authority)

PROBLEM 4.2: Implied Actual Authority

When its building needed painting, Church hired Bill to paint it. Church has hired Bill on various projects, including the last painting of the Church building. While working those projects, Bill had often asked his brother, Sam, to help out as needed. In fact, Sam had helped Bill with painting portions of the building that were very high and difficult for one person to paint. When it came time to paint those portions of the building, Bill asked for permission to hire another worker. Although the Church suggested that Bill might use Gary, who was hard to contract, Bill asked Sam to help out again. The morning that Bill and Sam came in to paint, Bill discovered that there wasn't enough paint, and sent same to the hardware store to purchase more paint. Does Sam have either express or implied authority to purchase the paint on behalf of the Church? How would you characterize such authority?

ANSWER:

1. Sam: he would have apparent authority to work on the church since he has done projects in the past and they have allowed him to do them. Sam doesn't have actual, but he has apparent. One could argue that he also has inherent since having paint to paint is inherent in the job as a painter.
2. Note: Sam is a subagent (see class notes pg 56): subagent has the same powers as an agent and has the duties of fidelity and care. So there is a line of continuity of agent to subagent.
    i. Two possible views
        1. The appointing agent has completed his task once the subagent is appointed and the subagent is now the only agent of the principle

    2. The appointing agent remains an agent of the principle but stays on as a principle to the subagent.
  ii. Termination: is made based upon manifestations of the parties, customs of the business, and all other circumstances.
  iii. L of agent for acts within authority: (duties)
    1. Restatement 2d 377: contractual duties: a person who makes a contract with another to perform services as an agent for him is subject to a duty to act in accordance with his promise.
    2. Restatement 2d 379: duty of care and skill: (see pg 185 supp):
        a. A paid agent is subject to a duty to the principle to act with a standard care, standard skill in the locality for the kind of work done, and exercise any special skills.
        b. An unpaid agent is under a duty to act with the same care and skill of non-agents performing small tasks.
3. Implied: type of actual authority circumstantially proven which are practically necessary to carry out duties actually delegated. Bill was hired to complete the paint job and had been allowed to get help from another person in the past. Arguably, he has implied actual authority for this paint job since the ceilings are high in some areas may require the work of two persons. However, the church suggested the use of Gary thus the church can argue that Bill only had authority to hire Gary and not some other person such as Sam. Since the fact pattern says that the church suggested Gary Bill could argue that the church meant he could have outside help not confined to only Gary.
4. Sam may not have expressed actual authority but implied actual authority
5. So once we determine Sam or Bill is w/in the church's authority, then that is the consent of the church. Agents have the incidental authority if it is w/in the scope of their employment. An extraordinary amount of paint or a truck would be different.

Agency & Partnership
SPARK LAW SERIES

6. Test for determining implied actual authority:
    iv. Rule: Whether the agent reasonably believes because of the present or past conduct of the principle that the principle wished him to act in a certain way or to have certain authority.
    v. Factors:
        1. Nature of task (It is difficult to paint ceiling by oneself, therefore it would seem logical to hire a sub-agent for help).
        2. Needed to carry out expressed authority (Bill had expressed authority to paint church).
        3. Similar past position (He did in the paint before and he got helped before).
        4. Specific past conduct by principle (The principle allowed him to hire someone else).
        5. Note: FYI: There is virtually always some implied authority

(4) Types of authority
    i. Actual: (1) an objective manifestation by the principle, (2) followed by the agent's reasonable interpretation of the manifestation, (3) which leads the agent to believe that it is authorized to act for the principle.
        1. Implied/incidental: authority to do acts which are incidental to it, usually accompany it, or are reasonably necessary to accomplish it.
        2. Express: (26) also
    ii. Apparent: the power to affect the legal relations of another person by transactions with third persons, professedly as agent for the other, arising from and in accordance with the other's manifestations to such third persons.
    iii. Estoppel
    iv. Inherent: (Catchall doctrine): neither actual nor apparent, estoppel doesn't apply.
        1. Two situations
            a. Certain unauthorized acts by agents

     b. Certain false representations of agent or apparent agent
  v. Ratify: the affirmance by a person of a prior act which did not bind him but which was done or professedly done on his account, whereby the act, as to some or all persons, is given effect as if originally authorized by him.

PROBLEM 4.3: Agent's Duty of Loyalty

ABC Corp. sold mobile homes and developed mobile home parks. ABC employed Agent, a licensed real estate broker, to acquire land for development as mobile home parks, at a weekly salary of $125. Agent told ABC that Parkacre was available for purchase. ABC asked Agent to purchase the land as a "straw man," and then to convey the land to ABC. Agent told ABC that the land would cost $30,000, and ABC gave Agent that amount.

Unknown to ABC, Agent had an interest in Parkacre. Before ABC had employed him, Agent had paid $1,000 for an option to buy Parkacre for $15,000. When ABC gave Agent the $30,000 he asked for, Agent exercised his option to buy Parkacre. Agent then used $14,000 of the $30,000 to complete the purchase, and kept the remaining $16,000.

ABC has now sued Agent for breach of fiduciary duty, asking that Agent be required to give ABC the entire $15,000 profit on the transaction. Agent argues that ABD's sole remedy is to rescind the transaction – return Parkacre in exchange for the $30,000 purchase price.

ANSWER:

(Same as Problem 1.2 – see above)

Restatement §390 – An agent who, to the knowledge of the principal, acts on the agent's own account in a transaction in which the agent is employed has a duty to deal fairly w/ the principal and to disclose to him all facts which the agent knows or should know would reasonably affect the principal's judgment, UNLESS the principal has manifested to the agent that the principal knows such facts or that the principal does not care to know them.

Additionally:
   a. Pay attention to Restatement §388 & §389 they are important.
   b. Under §390 the agent may with the consent of the principle may be able to disclose. But the agent still must disclose all material conduct.
   c. So in this problem the principle should prevail in almost any circumstances

Two Prongs to Fiduciary Duty:
   (1) Duty of care: skillfulness
   (2) Duty of loyalty: honesty

   Note: you cannot contract away the duty of loyalty. We can make specific exceptions but a general declaration is void against public policy.

Duty of Loyalty
   Res. 2d. § 387
      Agent must act solely for the benefit of the principal in all matters connected w/ the agency
      "punctilio of an honor most sensitive" (*Meinhard* Case)
   Res. 2d. § 388
      Agent must disclose all incidental profits to the principal from a transaction made for the principal and the principal has a right to these profits.
      Comment. b allows the agent to keep these if there is a custom or agreement.
      Notion that all funds that A hold in trust for P and must give over money. HE can deduct costs but here he did more than that since he made a large profit of 16k. This is where he breached his duty.
   Res 2d. § 389
      An agent cannot deal with the principal as an adverse party in any action connected with his agency without the principal's knowledge
      Harm to the principal is not relevant to this section

Agency & Partnership
SPARK LAW SERIES

Res. 2d § 390
> If the agent does act on his own account in a transaction with the principal he is under a duty to deal fairly with the principal and reveal all information which he should know would affect the principal's judgment unless the principal says he does not care

Res. 2d § 391
> Must disclose whether the agent represents an adverse party

Res. 2d § 392
> If agent does represent an adverse party they must disclose all relevant facts unless the principal says he knows or doesn't care to know

Res. 2d § 393
> Agent can't compete with the principal on his own time

Res. 2d. § 395, 396
> Agent cannot use confidential information of the principal even after the agency relationship is terminated

Res. 2d § 401
> Agent is liable from any loss caused by a breach of duty

Res. 2d. § 403
> If agent receives anything due to a violation of the duty of loyalty the principal has a right it to its value, or its proceeds

Res. 2d. § 404
> If a principal's asset is used for the profit of the agent he is liable to the principal for the value of its use.

Res. 2d. § 407
> Remedies
>> if the agent benefits, the principal can receive the benefit itself (he can get the money back itself), its value or proceeds and any additional damages caused by the breach.
>> if property is wrongfully disposed of the principal can only recover either its value or what the agent received

if the principal recovers from a 3rd person he can also recover any profit the agent improperly received

** these provisions generally allow the principal to be put back to a place better than where they started

---

PROBLEM 5.1: Apparent Authority

Palmer was planning to establish a dealership to sell farm machinery. He hired Adams to organize and operate the business. Adams was expressly authorized to collect for machinery sold and to hire and discharge office help, mechanics, and sales people but was expressly forbidden to borrow any money on Palmer's credit. Palmer supplied the money to establish the a bank account in the local bank. The account was in Palmer's name but Adams had authority to write checks on the account. From time to time, Adams overdrew the account, but Palmer had no knowledge or notice of the overdrafts. On each occasion, Adams made deposits to cover the overdraft. Subsequently, Palmer discharged Adams and learned for the first time that the account was overdrawn $2000. The bank brought an action to recover the amount of the overdraft from Palmer. May the bank recover? Give Reasons.

ANSWER:
1. Three (3) sources of Apparent Authority
   a. Direct communications from the principle to the 3rd party
   b. Appointment of an agent to a position by the principle – which stands for the notion that this person has the authority of persons who normally hold such position [CEO].
   c. Prior Act or Course of Dealing – notion in community that agent may establish reputation in community to have authority.

2. There is no actual authority; Adams was expressly forbidden to borrow on the acct. Further, there may apparent authority. The argument is that there is a course of dealing in the authority of Adams to write check. Adams may also argue that there was inherent authority because of the other

duties he held. Admittedly, there was there no direct communication from Palmer to the Bank (3rd party). But, Palmer is a general manager, which favors the Bank's position. But the Bank would have to know of the appointment and rely on it and reasonably interpret (b/c they are the 3rd party. Finally, there is a notion that the agent may have established a reputation in the community for this kind of authority.

Conclusion: Adams had the Apparent Authority because of check-writing. Palmer acquiesced b/c of not opening the bank statement to find out about the over draft. Just know the arguments for Adams ability to bind Palmer. Probably Palmer will be liable to the bank and Palmer would then have an action against Agent for breach of duty of loyalty and can get damages.

> Remedies: Res. 2d 407
>> if the agent benefits, the principal can receive the benefit itself (he can get the money back itself), its value or proceeds and any additional damages caused by the breach.

Agent Binding Principal through Unauthorized Acts
Apparent Authority Res. 2d. §27

- Principal holds out or indicates to 3rd party that agent has authority to act
- 3rd party has a duty to reasonably interpret principal's conduct, and actually, reasonably believe agent has the authority
- the reasonable belief might require inquiry if odd action
- Bank should have interpreted P's over drafted account as being conspicuous and should have put P on notice as to the overdrafts.

holding out by principal
- a stmt or message to community at large letting agent carryout unauthorized acts and not acting
- The manager had a duty to inquire about the account - which he didn't do.

Adams had authority to write checks on account, therefore the manager has a duty to check the account. If the manager was so concerned with the finances, he could have set up a system with the bank is which he could check all of the finances.

- not possible with an undisclosed principal agent showing 3rd party a written stmt by principal
- Agent had authority to write checks, but still he was expressly forbidden to borrow money on Palmer's credit.
- can be created by position Res. 2d § 49, 195
- applies to agents in the corporate context (officer)
- must show ordinary habits of persons in the locality and trade/profession
- will not cover extraordinary transactions

Focus on 3rd parties belief:

- Third party must know, must rely, and must reasonably interpret.
- agent can't create this unless they make a truthful stmt about authority and the authority is later changed
- the Res. does not require detrimental reliance but some jurisdictions do
- creates a valid and fully enforceable contract from all sides
- hiring an attorney does not create this

Inherent Agency Power

- Res. 2d. § 8A—derived solely from the agency relationship and exists to protect those who deal w/ agents
- §161 gives elements

Agency & Partnership
SPARK LAW SERIES

- Must be an agent of a partially or fully disclosed principal
- P is on the account and obviously principle
- Act done on principal's behalf
- A is authorized to write checks
- Act is incidental to or usually accompanies the authorized conduct
- 3rd party must reasonably believe agent was authorized
- The bank did believe.
- 3rd party must have no notice of lack of authority

The facts do not indicate that Palmer expressly let the bank know that the agent could not borrow credit on his account.

If Palmer wouldn't have expressly forbidden the overdrafts, A might be okay in the sense that principle should have given explicit instructions since lots of time the agent lacks financial wherewithal. Therefore, the principle would be in a better position to educate the agent. This would impose a duty to monitor.

PROBLEM 5.2: Estoppel

Merchant is in the business of selling, and of repairing used stereos. In the ordinary course of business, Buyer buys stereo from Merchant. Buyer pays Merchant the purchase price, and takes delivery of the stereo. Merchant later discovers that the stereo sold to Buyer was not owned by Merchant, but rather was owned by Owner. Suppose that Merchant acquired possession of the stereo in one of two different manners:

(1) Thief stole the stereo from Owner, and sold it to Merchant.
(2) Owner left the stereo with Merchant to be repaired.

Did Merchant have power to transfer to Buyer Owner's title to the stereo? If you believe that Merchant did have that power, what was its source – express authority, implied authority, apparent authority or estoppel to deny power? Explain.

ANSWER:

Since Owner never authorized Merchant to sell the stereo, Merchant never had <u>actual authority</u> (express or implied). Furthermore, there was no affirmative act on behalf of Owner to suggest that Merchant had <u>apparent authority</u> to sell the stereo. And lastly, since there was no misleading omission or conduct on behalf of Owner w/ the subsequent detrimental reliance by Buyer, there is no <u>estoppel</u>.

<u>What can Owner do if the stereo was **STOLEN**?</u>

Owner can try going after Merchant b/c he had no better title than the thief and therefore couldn't convey it. There was also no appearance of authority conveyed by Owner to sell the stereo. If M knew then M would be liable if he had reason to believe it was stolen. As a preventative measure M could have asked for a serial number and valid ID (they were in the best position to mitigate; he had the power to prevent).

Buyer, however, could argue <u>estoppel</u> b/c there was arguably an appearance of authority to sell the stereo since Merchant sold stereos in the ordinary course of business. But the <u>estoppel</u> argument also fail b/c there was no conduct or affirmative act that can be traced to Owner that gives Merchant the authority to sell. Therefore, O is estopped from going beyond merchant because we protect the BFP in good faith. We don't want to have to go after the person who bought in good faith.

<u>What can Owner do if he left the stereo to be REPAIRED and Merchant sold it?</u>

"Although mere possession and control of personal property are not ordinarily sufficient to estop the real owner from asserting his title against a person who has dealt w/ the one in possession on the faith of his apparent ownership, slight additional circumstances may turn the scale against the owner and estop him from asserting title against one who has purchased the property in good faith."

UCC 2-403 – any entrusting of possession of goods to a merchant who deals in goods of that kind gives him power to transfer all rights of the entrustor to a buyer in the ordinary course of business. This protects the Good Faith Buyer. This provision is harsher for the owner in (1).

So in either case the innocent buyer is ok. The real issue between the two boils down to the voluntary entrustment (if the stereo was being repaired).

Although under UCC 2-403 we have protection of a BFP in good faith, M is also liable to O under the CL principles of bailor-bailee. The true owner would have the best title against the world. The true owner has highest claim against others unless true owner abandons the right.

PROBLEM 5.11: *Agent Diversion of Funds*

Lawyer is a trial lawyer employed by Firm, which, through its lawyers, is engaged in the practice of law, specializing in general civil litigation. Lawyer is senior enough that Lawyer has the authority to accept new cases on behalf of the Firm.

Client hired Lawyer to represent her in a suit against Defendant. Even though Firm policy required only a $1500 retainer before accepting a new case, Lawyer asked for a $5000 retainer. When Client asked how to fill out the check Lawyer said that the Firm would stamp its name in

Agency & Partnership
SPARK LAW SERIES

as payee, so Client should leave the payee blank.

Unknown to Client, Lawyer was planning to leave the Firm, and didn't want Firm to know about Client's suit. Lawyer filled in the check by putting Lawyer's own name as payee. Lawyer then deposited the check in his personal bank account. Lawyer used the $5000 to finalize the arrangements for Lawyer's new office by paying the first month rent and security deposit. As Lawyer was driving home from signing the lease, he was killed in a car accident.

When Client inquired of the Firm about the status of the case, the Firm told her that it could not start work until Client paid the $1500 retainer. Client objected that Client had already paid $5000. May the Firm require Client to pay the $1500 retainer that it never received? If not, is the firm also subject to liability to Client for the additional $3500 demanded by lawyer solely for Lawyer's own purposes?

ANSWER: Lawyer (A) Firm (P), Client (3rd party)

> This is a close case. Investing is not what law firms do. But a retainer is part of the legal practice. From the plaintiff's side argue apparent authority (see sources under problem 5.1 above). We know there was actual authority to collect $1500 but not all $5000, so no actual authority. There is also a suggestion of inherent authority because of his position in the firm. Argue agency power, estoppel (that Client relied), or other variants. He did not spend must time on this one. [See other sections]
>
> Firm (principle) is responsible for the $1500. Firm expressly gave lawyer $1500 to retain as a retainer.
>
> The trickier part is the difference of $3500.
>
> Firm will argue $3500 was outside the scope of employment. However, client will argue apparent authority because lawyer (agent) could take money and deposit that is within the scope. Additionally, L's position as a firm representative gave him authority to take such

Agency & Partnership
SPARK LAW SERIES

money for a case and that this amount would not be extraordinary. The client (3rd party) must know that L had authority to take money, client relied on that authority, and 3.5k in excess will likely be reasonable. Reasonable reliance by the client. The firm however, could argue that the client hired the lawyer and not the firm.

Pertinent Code Sections
Apparent Authority Res. 2d. §27
- Principal holds out or indicates to 3rd party that agent has authority to act
- 3rd party has a duty to reasonably interpret principal's conduct, and actually, reasonably believe agent has the authority
- the reasonable belief might require inquiry if odd action

holding out by principal
- a statement or
- message to community at large
- letting agent carryout unauthorized acts and not acting
- not possible with an undisclosed principal
- agent showing 3rd party a written stmt by principal

can be created by position Res. 2d § 49, 195
- applies to agents in the corporate context (officer)
- must show ordinary habits of persons in the locality and trade/profession
- will not cover extraordinary transactions

Focus on 3rd party's belief
- agent can't create this unless they make a truthful statement about authority and the authority is later changed

Agency & Partnership
SPARK LAW SERIES

- the Res. does not require detrimental reliance but some jurisdictions do
- creates a valid and fully enforceable contract from all sides hiring an attorney does not create this
- Hiring an attorney does not mean that an attorney can do everything an attorney always does. Even though client hired lawyer and lawyers are allowed to get retainers but he was only supposed to take 1.5k. Just because L was hired doesn't mean that L can argue he had authority of any lawyer. He is still limited to ordinary matters in the locality limited by any instructions from the principle. Here he was authorized for 1.5k. But the client could reasonably rely on 5k as ordinary.

Inherent Agency Power
- Res. 2d. § 8A—derived solely from the agency relationship and exists to protect those who deal w/ agents

§161 gives the elements:
- must be an agent of a partially or fully disclosed principal
- act done on principal's behalf
- act is incidental to or usually accompanies the authorized conduct
- 3rd party must reasonably believe agent was authorized
- 3rd party must have no notice of lack of authority

Estoppel
- Based on 3rd party who changes position
- principal must have intentionally or carelessly caused belief, if principal knew of belief and its ramifications and fails to take reasonable steps to fix
- failure to act by principal is always enough
- can only be asserted by 3rd party
- possession of goods does not give power to transfer goods

Agency & Partnership
SPARK LAW SERIES

Section 219
When master is liable for the torts of his servants. (master: firm), lawyer (servant)

(1) A master is subject to liability for the torts of his servants committed while acting in the scope of their employment
(2) A master is not subject to liability for the torts of his servants acting outside the scope of their employment, unless:
  1. the master intended the conduct or the consequences, or
  2. The master was negligent or reckless, or
  3. The conduct violated a non-delegable duty of the master, or
  4. The servant purported to act or to speak on behalf of the principle and there was reliance upon apparent authority, or he was aided in accomplishing the tort by the existence of the agency relation.

Section 228 (scope pf employment)
(1) Conduct of servant is within the scope of employment if, but only if:
   a. It is a kind he is employed to perform;
   b. If occurs substantially within the authorized time and space limits;
   c. It is actuated, at least in part, by a purpose to serve the master, and
   d. If force if intentionally used by the servant against another, the use of force is not unexpected by the master.
(2) Conduct of the servant is not within the scope of employment if its is different in kind from the authorized, far beyond the authorized time or space limits, or too little actuated by a purpose to serve the master.

Section 229 (Kind of Conduct within scope of employment)

(1) To be within the scope of employment, conduct must be of the same general nature as that authorized, or incidental to the conduct authorized.
(2) In determining whether or not the conduct, although not authorized, is nevertheless so similar to or incidental to the conduct authorized as to be within the scope of employment, the following matters of fact are to be considered:
   a. Whether or not the act was one commonly done by such servants;
   b. The time, place and purpose of the act;
   c. The previous relations between the master and the servant.
   d. The extent to which the business of the master is apportioned between different servants.
   e. Whether or not the act is outside the enterprise of the master or, if within the enterprise, has not been entrusted to any servant;
   f. Whether or not the master has reason to expect that such an act will be done;
   g. The similarity in quality of the act done to the act authorized;
   h. Whether or not the instrumentality by which the harm is done has been furnished by the master to the servant;
   i. The extent of departure from the normal method of accomplishing an authorized result; and
   j. Whether or not the act is seriously criminal.

PROBLEM 6.1: *Partners as Agents*

Randy, Gus and Susan are partners conducting business under the name "Randy's Grocery Store." Because Randy and Susan have strong moral objections to the sale of alcoholic beverages, the partners agreed that Randy's would not do so. For many years Randy's never sold beer wine or liquor.

Recently, Randy's sales have been down. One day, Gus was in the store and noticed a lot of college T-shirts and Sweat-Shirts. Gus decided that Randy's could sell a lot of beer. Gus called up Spoetzel Brewing Co. and ordered several cases of "Shiner Bock" beer.

Agency & Partnership
SPARK LAW SERIES

When the beer was delivered, Randy was on the loading dock, and refused to accept the delivery. Spoetzel Brewing Co. sued Randy's and its partners for breach of contract. Randy's, Randy, Susan defend on two grounds. First, they argue that the partner's agreed that Randy's would not sell alcoholic beverages. Second, the argue that Randy's had never bought beer, wine, or liquor. What result? Would either of the following make any difference in your analysis?

(1) Spoetzel Brewing did not know that Gus was a partner in Randy's.
(2) It is common (or uncommon) for groceries in the area to sell beer.

Why or why not?

ANSWER:

1. The rule is partners <u>can</u> conduct businesses in the course of dealing. Here we see §301(1) pg 246 in supplement. Stores in this area do sell beer, so just because this store does not does not preclude liability. So it looks as though there is actual authority. But where there are specific limitations on obtaining actual authority, there is no actual authority. Randy and Susan expressly provided that there would not be alcohol sold. There is a good argument for apparent authority, even though there was not actual. 3rd parties are entitled to rely in apparent authority. Express partnership agreements are usually not asked for by third parties. In this case, there is no prior course of dealing so THERE CAN BE NO RELIANCE. There is a burden generally to check to see if a partnership exists. Public policy puts the burden on the party relying on authority (beer), however the beer company is only required to offer a rational basis for the assumption of authority. Either under implied actual authority or under apparent authority (because Gus was a general partner), there was express agreement that they would be partners. So Randy and Susan are liable on the contract. The statement of the partnership in the RUPA solidifies the authority. So in this

statement it may enlarge the covered actions by the partner. So a 3rd party could order the statement.
2. The character of business is an important variable; here it was a grocery store. The issue is whether selling beer is an ordinary part of the business:
    (1) For this business: if the county was dry then it wouldn't be a part of the business.
    (2) If the county is not dry, being that the grocery sells college merchandise it might be reasonable for the beer company to rely on the fact that it would be ordinary business were the grocery to sell beer. Since the grocery never bought beer before, they may have been on notice that this was a new product for the grocery. However, if the beer company didn't know it is likely that a court will be view this as reasonable reliance, especially since the beer company is not required to know about Randy's grocery, specifically only the general grocery business in which it is normal to sell beer. This policy enhances the flow of commerce.
    (3) 301(1): Each partner is an agent of the partnership for the purpose of its business. An act of a partner, including the execution of an instrument in the partnership name, for apparently carrying on in the ordinary course the partnership business or business of the kind carried on by the partnership binds the partnership, unless the partner has no authority to act for the partnership in the particular matter and the person with whom the partner was dealing knew or had received a notification that the partner lacked authority.
        a. Comment: 301(1) effects two changes from UPA Sec 9(1). First, it clarifies that a partner's apparent authority includes acts for carrying on in the ordinary course "Business of the kind carried on by the partnership," not just business of the particular partnership in question. The UPA is ambiguous at this.

Agency & Partnership
SPARK LAW SERIES

PROBLEM 6.3: Management and Conduct of Firm Business/Estoppel

Ole consents to Lena telling Finn that Ole and Lena are partners in the practice of law (which they are not). Believing that he is dealing w/ Lena and Ole as partners, Finn lends money to Lena to buy a law library.
  a. Is Ole subject to liability to Finn for the loan to Lena?
  b. Would it make any difference in your answer if Lena instead borrowed money for the purpose of buying a sports car? Office supplies?

ANSWER:

UPA section & Rules for Determining the Existence of a partnership

UPA section 16 Partner by Estoppel
 § 16. Partner by Estoppel
  (1) When a person, by words spoken or written or by conduct, represents himself, or consents to another representing him to any one, as a partner in an existing partnership or with one or more persons not actual partners, he is liable to any such person to whom such representation has been made, who has, on the faith of such representation, given credit to the actual or apparent partnership, and if he has made such representation or consented to its being made in a public manner he is liable to such person, whether the representation has or has not been made or communicated to such person so giving credit by or with the knowledge of the apparent partner making the representation or consenting to its being made.
   (a) When a partnership liability results, he is liable as though he were an actual member of the partnership.
   (b) When no partnership liability results, he is liable jointly with the other persons, if any, so consenting to the contract or representation as to incur liability, otherwise separately.
  (2) When a person has been thus represented to be a partner in an existing partnership, or with one or more persons not actual partners, he is an agent of the persons consenting to such representation to bind them to the same extent and in the same manner as though he were a partner in fact, with

respect to persons who rely upon the representation. Where all the members of the existing partnership consent to the representation, a partnership act or obligation results; but in all other cases it is the joint act or obligation of the person acting and the persons consenting to the representation.

Revised Uniform Partnership [RUPA]

SECTION 308. LIABILITY OF PURPORTED PARTNER.

(a) If a person, by words or conduct, purports to be a partner, or consents to being represented by another as a partner, in a partnership or with one or more persons not partners, the purported partner is liable to a person to whom the representation is made, if that person, relying on the representation, enters into a transaction with the actual or purported partnership. If the representation, either by the purported partner or by a person with the purported partner's consent, is made in a public manner, the purported partner is liable to a person who relies upon the purported partnership even if the purported partner is not aware of being held out as a partner to the claimant. If partnership liability results, the purported partner is liable with respect to that liability as if the purported partner were a partner. If no partnership liability results, the purported partner is liable with respect to that liability jointly and severally with any other person consenting to the representation.

(b) If a person is thus represented to be a partner in an existing partnership, or with one or more persons not partners, the purported partner is an agent of persons consenting to the representation to bind them to the same extent and in the same manner as if the purported partner were a partner, with respect to persons who enter into transactions in reliance upon the representation. If all of the partners of the existing partnership consent to the representation, a partnership act or obligation results. If fewer than all of the partners of the existing partnership consent to the representation, the person acting and the partners consenting to the representation are jointly and severally liable.

(c) A person is not liable as a partner merely because another in a statement of partnership authority names the person.

Agency & Partnership
SPARK LAW SERIES

(d) A person does not continue to be liable as a partner merely because of a failure to file a statement of dissociation or to amend a statement of partnership authority to indicate the partner's dissociation from the partnership.

(e) Except as otherwise provided in subsections (a) and (b), persons who are not partners as to each other are not liable as partners to other persons.

Under both of the statutes must have

   (i) Holding out or representation by words or conduct that a particular person is a partner

   (ii) Holding out requires a 3rd party extension of credit to the actual or apparent partnerships on faith of such representation

   (iii) Requires a reliance on the purported partnership relationship → must be relied on by the 3rd party credit extension influenced by the credit extension of the 3rd party to the partner. Partnership status is determined by looking at one who held out to be a partner in a joint venture then there is a purported partnership and a purported partner

Ole, Lena, Finn

- Finn lent money to apparent partnership. Who is liable if a sports car is purchased? Ole, Lina or both. Contrast with office supplies on open account → go through Estoppel analysis. Ole is estopped from saying that there is no partnership
- As long as there is holding out as partners then is it irrelevant the ordinary course of business.
- Partnership by Estoppel treat as if actually a partnership given same rule to apply partners are bound with regards to usual and customary in the business. This puts the relationship in the nature of an ordinary partnership but they are not bound in regards to transactions that are outside the ordinary course of business
- For the sports car that is not reasonable part of business. The Sports car is a stretch. Reasonable reliance relates to the ordinary business. Here a law library and office supplies would be ordinary business however, a sports car would likely not be in the ordinary business since lawyers do not usually use partnership money to buy a firm car and even if they did a sports car might be excessive

Agency & Partnership
SPARK LAW SERIES

and outside of scope, unreasonable to rely on, given the business itself. RELIANCE IS WHAT IS THE HOOK
- Therefore, for part A: they are all liable.
- For part B:
- This is arguably a private representation and thus requires direct or actual reliance. The threshold for public representation is not as high. If actual reliance cannot be shown, then there will not be liability.
- O can argue that he is not liable because he only consented to the partnership and did not a role in holding out.

Notes

1. Partnership by Estoppel –
   a. What are the legal ramifications for purported partners?
   b. UPA §7(1) → §16(1) then to – RUPA at §308(e) is the same
      1) Under the old statute it requires a holding out or representation by words or conduct that a particular person is a partner. This older section also requires a 3rd party extension of credit to the partnership of faith of such representation made to them. It requires a reliance on the purported partnership relationship by the party extending credit.
      2) Under §308 – the purported partner (holding out is the joint venture of the purported partnership and the purported partner). Now these principles both obtain to partnership and purported partnership. So you could have A & B be a partnership. And they may hold out C as being a partner. And C may participate. Or we could have A & B & C not thinking they are a partnership but they are holding out as such then the liability principles are the same.
   c. So in this problem OLE consents to LENA that they are partnership, they is so they can pay the loan. There is good reason to do this, the loan security, or interest rate charged is helpful. This holding out make the partnership look larger than it actually is. Finn lent money for the purpose of purchasing a law library? Who is liable OLE? LENA? Or both?

Agency & Partnership
SPARK LAW SERIES

1) First go through estoppel analysis and say OLE is estopped from asserting non-existence of the partnership since Finn relied on the reason for lending the money. But if they purchased a sports car that is not is the course of business.

This is a partnership by estoppel, which means you treat it as though it were a partnership. So the partnership and partners are bound by obligations customary in their course of business. The liability principles are no broader under a partnership by estoppel, they are the same. Here the sports car is a stretch.

PROBLEM 6.4: *Liability*

Odo and Word are partners in the investment banking business. Odo and Worf both consent to Basheer holding himself out as their partners to Dax. Apparently acting for partnership purposes, Basheer borrows money from Dax who thinks she is lending to the partnership.

(1) Who is liable on the loan?
(2) Would it make any difference to your answer if Odo, but not Worf, consented to being held out?
(3) Would it make any difference in your answer if Worf had consented to Basheer holding himself as a partner to Quark, but had never consented to any holding out to Dax?

(1) They all are liable.
- This is arguably a private representation and thus requires direct or actual reliance. The threshold for public representation is not as high. If actual reliance cannot be shown, then there will not be liability.
-

Agency & Partnership
SPARK LAW SERIES

PROBLEM 6.5: *Management and Conduct of Firm Business/Estoppel*

With the consent of Dick, Jane holds herself out to Emily as being a partner of Dick's. Emily signs a contract to sell widgets to what she believes is the Dick and Jane partnership on open account. Before Jane delivers the widgets, Dick tell her that there is no partnership and tells her that he will not be liable for the contract. Assuming the transaction is one that would have bound the partnership if made by a partner.
    a. Under UPA §16 may Emily bring an action for breach of contract against Dick?
    b. Could Emily do so under RUPA §308?

<u>**ANSWER:**</u>

- Partners can bind the partnership with regards to ordinary partnership business and all partners are liable for ordinary business liabilities.
- Jane is a purported partner
- Issue: Is this engagement with Emily binding on Dick
- This case analysis follows section 308

<u>The statutory test for partnership by estoppel requires that</u>:
(1) Credit must have been extended on the basis of partnership representation or
(2) That the alleged partner must have made or consented to representation being made in a public manner whether or not such representations being made in a public manner or whether or not such representations were actually communicated to the person extending credit. This is the common law test as codified.

- However, the last part of (a) seems to extend liability beyond the common law test of reliance if the representation is made in a public manner.
- Still, the court reasons that even with the statutory enactment that such a departure from well a developed common law doctrine as the foundation of estoppel is that one is bound by saying or doing something upon which another relies to his or her detriment.

Agency & Partnership
SPARK LAW SERIES

- Looking again at 308 (a) relating to public representation is seems that it does not remove the requirement of reliance after consider the language of B. When a person has been thus represented to be a partner in an existing partnership he is an agent of the person consenting to such representation to bind them to the same extent as if he were a partner who respect to any who rely on the representation.
- The word thus is a reference back to subsection (a) Accordingly, under subsection (b) even when the representation has been made in a public manner the purported partners are bund only to person who rely upon the representation. It would be remarkable to require reliance under subsection B but not under A.
- Still in the best reading of (a) "if he has made such representation or consented to its being made in a public manner he is liable to such person. Who is such person? The obvious candidate is the person described earlier in the sentence; a person "to whom such representation has been made, who has on the faith of such representation, given credit to the actual or apparent partnership. In other words such person is one who has relied on the representation. The purported partner is liable only to one who has relied.

Section 16 UPA elements
  (i) Hold yourself out as a partner
  (ii) Purported partner has to know that you are holding yourself out as a partner
  (iii) Reliance
  (iv) Given credit → has credit been extended here? Before Jane delivers widgets he tells her that there is no partnership. If delivery had to be paid for then there would have been an extension of credit.

  <u>16 limitation</u> → partner and purported partner liable on the contract as no partnership has resulted see 16 (b) UPA

Revised Uniform Partnership 308

Only restates the UPA. Argument against literal interpretation with such a firm well respected rule from common law is that before being made part the legislature statement under section 16 comment that should expressly state that a change in the law is meant. Can be argued both

Agency & Partnership
SPARK LAW SERIES

ways as between the two if had to rule then rule that estopell basis can be used in absence of extension of credit as otherwise there is no liability. In the 308 section one only need to enter into the transaction to have liability credit extension is not needed.

NOTES
1. This is a purported partnership question. Jane is a purported partner. The question is whether this engagement she entered into with Emily binds Dick. Under §16 there are elements, which must be satisfied. (See above) Specifically, the extension of credit is in question. Before Jane delivers the widgets, there is no extension of credit. After deliver, there is an extension of credit. This illustrates the difference between a partner and a purported partner. The purported partner cannot create liability for the partnership or the partner.
2. Under RUPA §308 – here entering into a transaction is enough to bind. The comment in §308 says there should be no change between the UPA and RUPA. The second argument is that with such a firm and well-respected rule in common law, the comment should express that there is a change.

So the answer here is that under §308 it could be argued either way. Carson says he would likely side with an estoppel base argument. "So in the absence of an actual extension of credit, there should be no liability. Know that there is no argument under §16 of UPA. TX retains the extension of credit requirement.

PROBLEM 6.6: *Partners as Managers*

The question is too long to write. It is about Mathew Emily and Paul opening a new grocery store called MEP Grocers. The have no

Agency & Partnership
SPARK LAW SERIES

partnership agreement except as to division of equal profits. The issue centers on Matthew contracting to sell bread. Here our my notes (hope this is not on the exam, but there should be several small questions):

ANSWER:

A. Problem 6.6
1. MEP is liability to both stores under Apparent Authority. All P has to do is prove there is a partnership, then D shows that P knew, the P shows that did not have knowledge of the agreement obtaining actual authority. The Contract to Emily, they are liable.
2. "Partners vote 2:1 to buy bread....→ must inform
    - The contract to emily- they are liable. The default rule is that they have authority since they are agents and there is not agreement ot limit their authority. Buying bread in an ordinary businsess transaction for the grocery. All partners are liable for partner losses nad profits, so Emily would have a right to indemnification. Because there is no dispute at this time, they will not be liable to each other for any breach of duties as partersn because all aprtners have an equal right to manage the partnership unde UPA §18(e).

    Under partnership law, you may dissolve at any time even if contravention of the agrmt, but there would be a breach of K claim against Matthew. This is effective to all who have notice. You cannot dissove retroactivley, you only stop liability for *Future* transactions if you know you will resign & deal will come thru. If you are a partner at the time of the K, you are bound. Thus, the only remedy is to dissolve the p'ship & inform Wholesome.

B. Mattew contract with Arrow who has no knowledge of the vote, is MEP liable? Yes, there is not actual authority, but there is with regard to arrow if there is no vote, the basis for liablity will be the apparent authority. Do we still have breach of duty by Matthew?

Agency & Partnership
SPARK LAW SERIES

3. After losing the vote, Matt contracts to buy bread again for Arrow.

   Assume Arrow doesn't know of partner's vote.
   a. Are either MEP Grocers, Emily, or Paul subject to liability to Arrow on account of the contract?
      i. They are probably going to be on hook on the contract because they have apparent authority.
      ii. They are relying on default rule that partners are general agents and do not have knowledge that the agency was destroyed by the vote
   b. Matthew would be liable to partnership and other partners for this action because Matthew breached the duty of loyalty to the partnership.

Problem 6.6
- Matt, Emily, and Paul are partners
- Have no written or oral agreement as to business or affairs
   1. Without first discussing matter, Matt contacts Arrow bread and contracted for Arrow to sell bread for a week. At the same time, Paul contracted w/ wholesome bakers for purchase of bread for month.
      c. Is partnership subject to liability to arrow or wholesome
         i. Liable to both, all partners are agents for the conduct of partnership business, partnership is liable and partner is liable to both
      d. As among partners, are either Matt or Paul liable to Emily or to MEP for contracting for purchase of bread w/out consulting other partners?
         i. They have authority, they are not liable to either Emily or MEP
         ii. Are you left w/ default rule then?
         iii. There is no agreement limiting ability
      e. Suppose Emily has to pay, these deliveries are made and the bills are never paid, and they hit up Emily for the bill, would Matt or Paul be liable to her?
         i. They are on the hook for partner share profits and losses
         ii. So it would follow she has the right of indemnifaication to the other partners for their share.

Agency & Partnership
SPARK LAW SERIES

2. Partners meet to discuss, Emily and Paul likes wholesome, Matt likes Arrow, Emily and Paul like Wholesome. Matt writes Wholesome letter denying authority of Emily and Paul and disclaim liability on new purchases from wholesome
    a. Grocer is liable and matt is liable. Partners maintain accounts within the scope of the partnership, but the partnership can and often does own property. So, under revised act, must first sue partnership, then sue any or all partners
    b. If partnership has no assets and are unable to satisfy claim, then you are able to go after any and all of the partners
    c. One reason for partnerships is partnership property generally speaking may not be looked to by third parties to satisfy the personal debts of any partner
    d. You can always go after the partnership for partnership debts, but you cannot pursue the partnership for the individual obligations for partners that do not arise out of partnership interests.
    e. Thus, you cannot seize partnership property to collect a partner's debt, but you can receive the partner's draw from the partnership
    f. What action could Matt take to avoid liability of purchase to Wholesome?
        i. He can dissolve the partnership
        ii. Under partnership law, you may dissolve partnership at any time
        iii. But after the delivery of bread and completion of contract, you cannot dissolve the partnership and are bound
        iv. Thus if you are a partner at the time of the contract, then you are bound to that contract
    g. What are the chances Matt will pay wholesome entire amount of claim?
        i. You could probably figure out some defenses
        ii. So Matt is probably would have to pay, but probably not pay the full amount
        iii. He needs to decide whether the retention of an attorney would be cost effective rather than just paying
        iv. Some liability and exposure

Agency & Partnership
SPARK LAW SERIES

3. After losing the vote, Matt contracts to buy bread again for Arrow. Assume Arrow doesn't know of partner's vote.
   a. Are either MEP Grocers, Emily, or Paul subject to liability to Arrow on account of the contract?
      i. They are probably going to be on hook on the contract because they have apparent authority.
      ii. They are relying on default rule that partners are general agents and do not have knowledge that the agency was destroyed by the vote
   b. Matthew would be liable to partnership and other partners for this action because Matthew breached the duty of loyalty to the partnership.

4. Suppose Matt knows Paul want to buy bread from Wholesome, and before they talk to Emily, Matt orders from Arrow
   a. They are liable to both Arrow and Wholesome because there has been no limitation as to their agency duties yet. In the absence of the vote and Arrow knowing about the conflict, the general rule that partners are general agents still applies to Arrow and Wholesale.
      i. The court would likely find apparent authority with regard to the third party and arrow will lose
      ii. In all of these, the third party is out of it, and advances thrust to facilitate business
      iii. We keel the third party out of these disputes and we don't want the third party to hire detectives.
   b. As amongst the partners, there is probably a breach claim and there is an implied implicit understanding that nothing be done until they resolve the conflicting views.
   c. As a matter of proof, it is much more difficult than if you have the former votes

You have an argument of deniability, understanding that until we actually made a decision, the status quo would occur

---

PROBLEM 6.7: Limited Liability Companies

Lucy is member of Belle's Ice Cream Shop, LLC, a member-managed limited liability company organized under the ULLCA. The LLC has two other members, Mary and Paula.

Agency & Partnership
SPARK LAW SERIES

The LLC holds title in its name to a building just off the town square in Sealy, which it has been using to operate a small ice cream shop under the name "Belle's". Business had turned down in Sealy. Believing that Belle's would do better in nearby Brenham, Lucy asked the neighbor, who owner the store next door, if he was interested in buying the building and lot. Lucy and Neighbor agreed to a price of $250,000. Neighbor paid Lucy the $250,000, and Lucy signed, acknowledged and delivered a Deed transferring the LLC's interest in the building and lot. Lucy had never discussed a possible sale w/ Mary or Paula, and did not have their consent to a sale of the property.

Mary and Paula have asked you if they may recover the property.

a. Assuming that the articles of organization of the LLC have no provisions that might affect your answer, please advise Mary and Paula, giving reasons to support your answer. (*See* ULLCA §§301, 404(c))
b. Would your answer change if Lucy, Mary and Paula had been operating Belle's Ice Cream Shop as a partnership under the UPA? (*See* UPA §§9, 10, 18. As a partnership under the RUPA? *See* RUPA §§301, 302, 401).

ANSWER:

Under 404 (c) 12 would need consent from rest of members as this sale of property
Under 301 (c) a member under a member management company can transfer the property
404 (c) 12 trumps 301 (c) as one may not convert in this case w/o consent of the partners as doing so would take away their investment. A member may convey real property pursuant to 301 (c) in light of the 404 c (12) prohibition in transferring property without consent if the transfer of the property would represent transferring all of the assets then must have consent of the partners/members

Agency & Partnership
SPARK LAW SERIES

Can the partnership/company get the property back?
Section 301 (2) RUPA and UPA 9 (2) gives the same answer thepartnership is not bound

Under ULLCA member may convey the property even if violates the law and an agreement among the parties Pursuant to 301 (c) this provision provides actual authority for members to convey the property subject to 404 (c) (12) exception and the transaction will be valid so long as they don't convey everything.

If third party is given notice of the partners restriction as the partner has actual authority to conduct the sale then the 3rd party might have to give the real estate back but 3rd party is under no obligation to do so.

LLC holds title to building and is being used to operate ice cream shop. Lucy is member of LLC. Two other members, Mary or Paula
-Thinking you could do better elsewhere, Lucy sells to Neighbor w/out knowledge of Mary or Paula.
-Under §301 of ULLCA, members of LLC are agents for ordinary course of business
-§ 404(c)(12) with regard to extraordinary matters, you need unanimity, unless you have an agreement otherwise
-Very essential functions of actions and conduct require unanimity
-Same w/ regard to partnership matters for your practice
-If there is a small handful, identity of members is very important
-Is less important in large sweatshops
-Once you increase the numbers, you decrease the possibilities of unanimity
    -You may have a super-super majority requirement
    -80-90% is necessary to make extraordinary deals
-The rules of the statute is extraordinary matters require unanimity
-All or substantially all of the assets is extraordinary matter
-The building for retail purposes will be all or substantially all
-If the partnership had one million dollars of CDs in Swiss bank, don't have sale of all or substantially all of the assets.

-Would answer change if they operated under a partnership?
    -Under both partnership law and LLC law, you need general agency and general agency
        in LLC where members rule

Agency & Partnership
SPARK LAW SERIES

-That can be limited even w/ regard to ordinary matters if there is a majority
-Ordinary matters, the general agency for each either member or partner can be effectively countermanded by a vote and notice to the third party
-Under both forms, extraordinary matters must be decided by unanimous vote of the group
-Rule is designed to facilitate commerce
-Every time you buy computer from computer company, shouldn't need 40 pages of documentation
-IF clerk shouldn't sell for right amount of money, third party can go about business
-In extraordinary matters, even the third party needs to know who has the authority to go through with the deal- must have actual authority, apparent authority will not work
-Because in extraordinary matters, the costs to investigate are incidental to the costs of the matter

Managerial Discretion and Fiduciary Duties
    A.   Business Judgment Rule
        1.   General Principal

Restatement (Second of Agency) Section 387
    Unless otherwise agreed, an agent is subject to a duty to his principal to act solely for the benefit of the principal in all matters connected with his agency

    Unless otherwise agreed, a paid agent is subject to a duty to the principal to act with standard care and with the skill which is the standard in the locality for the kind of work which the agent is employed to perform and, in addition, to exercise any special skill that the agent has.

Fiduciary duty has two major prongs
    (1)   Care
    (2)   Loyalty
Fiduciary duty arises out of:
    (1)   Relationship between the parties
    (2)   Control over property or other interests that are to be exercised for the benefit others.

Agency & Partnership
SPARK LAW SERIES

PROBLEM 7.2: Business Judgment Rule [Duty of Care]

Mt. Hood Meadows, Oreg., Ltd. is a limited partnership established to carry on the business of constructing and operating a winter sports development. Under the limited partnership agreement, management of the business and affairs of Mt. Hood Meadows is the responsibility of its general partner, Mt. Hood Meadows Development Corp. That agreement also provides that the limited partners have no right to take part in the control of the business. For the year in which profits were earned after 1974, the general partner elected to distribute only 50% of the limited partner's taxable profits. The remaining profits were retained and reinvested in the business. Three of the limited partners have sued to force the general partners to distribute the retained profits.

Assume that the limited partnership agreement does not require the distributions, and that they are not required under the applicable statute. On what basis, if any, should a court interfere in the general partner's decision as to the distributions of profits?

ANSWER:

General rule- general partner's decision should stand in the absence of circumstance; the limited partners have no right of control over the partnership

1. Any relief in this case available for the Limited Partners? –
    a. The matter is not dispositive under contract. That is a better place for specific problems or concerns, like problems. MBCA – §7.32 – this applies, without it any K trying to limit the B/D is void. It initially has to be unanimous but it can be amended later. Control is among GP. With LLC, LP, LLP – those frame works are default rules, the PARTNERSHIP agmt can provide otherwise. Now that is not unrestricted, but it is very

broad. Here we simply have a disagreement about policy, but policy is to be dictated by the B of D. GP has fid duties to LP, but GP is essentially under the Bz judgment rule. There is a disagreement about policy, but that is set by GP. Find out who dictates policy, GP or B of D, probably both, and specifically not LPs.

b. The RUPA and LPA (1976) – have commentary in several places, which expressly states that the principles are borrowed from Corporate law.

c. Is the threshold issue who has authority to make distribution? Well 1st find out whether you are dealing with the default rules. 2nd what are the default rules 3rd what is the applicability of the business judgment rule

d. Under RUPA §4.04(e) – A partner owes a duty of care to the partnership and the other partners to act in the conduct of the business of the partnership in a manner that does not constitute gross negligence or willful misconduct. An error in judgment or a failure to use ordinary care is not gross negligence

e. Note: Many of the sources for the business judgment rule are admittedly derived from corporate law. See Text page 359, "As applied in evaluating the decisions of corporate officers or directors, the business judgment rule protects them from liability on account of business judgments made in good faith:

> A director or officer who makes a business judgment in good faith fulfills his duty [of care] IF:
> (i) he is not interested in the subject of his business (no self-dealing)
> (ii) he is informed with respect to the subject of his business judgment to the extent he reasonably believes necessary; and
> (iii) he rationally believes that his business judgment is in the best interest of the corporation

Agency & Partnership
SPARK LAW SERIES

PROBLEM 7.4: Duty of Loyalty

Covalt and High were corporate officers and shareholders in Concrete Systems, Inc. (CSI). Covalt owned 25% of the stock and High owned the remaining 75% of the stock. Both men received remuneration from CSI in the form of salaries and bonuses.

In late 1971, after both High and Covalt had become corporate officers of CSI, they formed a partnership. The partnership bought land and built an office and warehouse building. In Feb 1973, CSI leased the building from the partnership for a five-year term. Following the expiration of the initial term of the lease, CSI remained a tenant of the building; the corporation and the partnership orally agreed to certain rental increases. The corporation made substantial improvements to the leasehold. Under the original lease any improvements to the premises were to accrue to the premises were to accrue to the partnership upon termination of the lease.

In Dec, 1978, Covalt resigned his position as an officer of CSI and went to work for one of its competitors. Covalt, however, remained a partner w/ High in the ownership of the land and the building rented to CSI. On Jan 9, 1979, Covalt wrote to High demanding that the monthly rent for the partnership real estate leased to CSI be increased from $1,850 to $2,850 per month. High refused to increase the rent and took no action to renegotiate the amount of the monthly rent payable.

Question: Assuming that $2,850 was the fair rental value of the land and building, has he breached his fiduciary?

   Duty as a partner?

ANSWER:

RUPA §404(b) & UPA §21
High owed his Covalt, his partner, a fiduciary duty, which necessarily encompasses the duty of exercising good faith, honesty, and fairness

Agency & Partnership
SPARK LAW SERIES

in his dealings with him and the funds of the partnership. The fiduciary duty exists concurrently with the obligations set forth in the partnership agreement whether or not expressed in them. In any fiduciary relationship, the burden of proof shifts to the fiduciary to show by clear and convincing evidence that a transaction is equitable and just. Where there is a question of breach of a fiduciary duty of a managing partner, all doubts will be resolved against him, and the managing partner has the burden of proving his innocence.

An agreement entered into that results in no fiduciary duty of the managing general partner is void as violative of public policy. Fiduciary duty of loyalty remains and into not extinguished by contract unless a specific matter is waived after full disclosure and the other parties is notified of the ability to have counsel present.

Here, assuming that the $2,850 was fair rental value, High had a duty of loyalty to the partnership w/ Covalt and he breached that duty by not taking the offer. The offer was in the best interest of the partnership.

PROBLEM 8.1: *Firm's Accountability (Agent issues)*

Firm's Accountability for Notification to and Knowledge of the Agent

Tom and Paul are partners in Law Firm. Tom and Paul agree that Tom will act as managing partner. As such, Tom handles all administrative and personnel matters.

On repeated occasion, Paul sees Associate, during the normal course of a working day, become unreasonably angry with secretaries and paralegals. Paul always admonished Associate to act in a more appropriate manner, but did not report Associate's conduct to Tom. Several months later, Associate becomes angry, and hits Clerk.

Clerk has now sued Law Firm, claiming that Law Firm knew of Associate's explosive tendencies and negligently failed to either fire or control Associate. In Clerk's suit, will Law Firm be responsible for Paul's knowledge? See UPA §12, RUPA §102(f). Compare, ULLCA §102.

Agency & Partnership
SPARK LAW SERIES

ANSWER:

UPA §12: Notice to any partner (in this case Paul) of any matter relating to partnership affairs (Associate was unreasonably angry with secretaries and paralegals), and the knowledge of the partner acting in the particular matter, acquired while a partner or then present to his mind (Paul actually sees Associate), and the knowledge of any other partner who reasonably could and should have communicated it to the acting partner (Paul could have told Tom but did not), operate as notice to or knowledge of the partnership (therefore this acts as notice to Tom through Paul's knowledge), except in the case of a fraud on the partnership committed by or with the consent of that partner (unless it can be shown that this was fraud on the partnership done by Paul or consented by Paul).

Therefore in this situation, the Law Firm will be responsible for Paul's knowledge.

RUPA §102(f): A partner's knowledge (is cognitive awareness), notice (is less than knowing and is based on a person's actual knowledge, receipt of a notification or reason to know based on actual knowledge of other facts and the circumstances at the time), or receipt of a notification of a fact relating to the partnership is effective immediately as knowledge by (Paul, the partner had knowledge because he actually saw this), notice to, or receipt of a notification by the partnership, except in the case of a fraud on the partnership committed by or with the consent of that partner.

Therefore it is deemed that the Law Firm had knowledge through Paul, and therefore may be liable.

ULLCA §102:
(a) a person knows a fact if the person has actual knowledge of it.
(b) a person has notice of a fact if the person:
   (1) knows the fact;
   (2) has received a notification of the fact; or

(3) has reason to know the fact exists from al of the facts known tot he person at the time in question.
(c) A person notifies or gives a notification of a fact to another by taking steps reasonably required to inform the other person in ordinary course, whether or not the other person knows the fact.
(d) A person receives a notification when the notification:
   (1) comes to the person's attention; or
   (2) is duly delivered at the person's place of business or at any other place held out by the person as a place for receiving communications.
(e) An entity knows, has notice, or receives a notification of a fact ... when the individual conducting the transaction for the entity knows ... or in any event when the fact would have been brought to the individual's attention had the entity exercised reasonable diligence. An entity exercises reasonable diligence if it maintains reasonable routines for communicating significant information to the individual conducting the transaction for the entity and there is reasonable compliance with the routines. Reasonable diligence does not require an individual acting for the entity to communicate information unless the communication is part of the individual's regular duties or the individual has reason to know of the transaction and that the transaction would be materially affected by the information.

Therefore, had the entity performed reasonable diligence, then they will be deemed to have knowledge. But what is reasonable diligence, when they maintain reasonable routines for communicating significant information to the individual acting for the entity (Tom) and there is reasonable compliance. So had the entity established a routine where partners would communicate to the controlling partner like Tom, the Law Firm will be deemed to have known. So unless Paul had as part of his duties to communicate Associates behavior, the Law Firm will not be deemed to have knowledge.

PROBLEM 8.3: *Time from which Notification of Knowledge Affects Principal*

Owner owns and operates Mall. Alan and Betty are leasing agents for the Mall and share an office suite in the Mall. As such, each is authorized to negotiate and to sign, on Owner's behalf, leases covering space in the Mall. On Friday, Betty leased space to Laser, who

Agency & Partnership
SPARK LAW SERIES

planned to open a laser-tag game in the Mall.

Unknown to Betty, on Monday, Alan had leased space in the Mall to Arcade, who planned to open a video arcade in the Mall. As a condition for signing the lease, Arcade insisted on the inclusion of an "exclusivity provision" under which Owner agreed not to lease space in the Mall to any other arcade or amusement center. Alan forgot to tell either Owner of Betty about the exclusivity provision included in Arcade's lease.

Question: Assume that Alan had authority to agree to the inclusion of the exclusivity provision, and that Owner will be liable to Arcade for breach of contract. Assume further that Owner will also be liable for special damages if it knowingly breached the lease w/ Arcade. Will Owner be responsible for special damages?

ANSWER:

Alan, an agent for Owner, has complete authority to bind Owner. Since Alan knew about the contract provision, that knowledge can be imputed to Owner, the principal. The doctrine of Imputed Knowledge involves holding a principal to the wrongs committed by his agent. This doctrine draws its sources from the law of respondeat superior. The expectation interest of the other party is irrelevant in an impute knowledge context b/c the knowledge at issue is acquired by the agent through means other than a deliberate effort by the other party to convey info to the principal.

R2d §381

This knowledge is "imputed" to the principal b/c the agent has a duty to convey it to him. "Unless otherwise agreed, an agent is subject to a duty to use reasonable efforts to give his principal info which is relevant to affairs entrusted to him and which, as the agent has notice, the principal would desire to have and which can be communicated w/o violating a superior duty to a third person."

The only EXCEPTION to the imputed knowledge doctrine is the

Agency & Partnership
SPARK LAW SERIES

Adverse Interest doctrine. Under this exception, if an agent is acting adversely to the principal and entirely for his own or another's purposes, his knowledge is <u>not imputed</u>. The fact, however, that an agent has conflicting goals (like a desire to earn commission and thus keep silent about an outstanding equity) will not rise to the level of an adverse interest. It is only when the agent totally abandons the principal's business, such as taking a bribe to keep quiet, that the knowledge will not be imputed.

An EXCEPTION to the Adverse Interest Exception is the <u>Sole Actor Rule</u>. This rule applies when the agent, even though clearly acting as an adverse party to the principal by, for example, selling some of his own property to the principal, also receives that property in the capacity of agent for the principal and is the only agent acting in that capacity. His knowledge as agent, is imputed to the principal but not his knowledge pertaining to his adverse interest.

PROBLEM 9.1; *Ratification of Unauthorized Transactions [Affirmance]*

Allen, purporting to represent Paula but without authority or power to bind, leases Paula's farm to Terry for a term of five years. Allen tells Paula what he has done, but does not tell her the term of the lease. Without inquiring as to the lease term, Paula demands, and accepts from Terry, the security deposit and first month's rent. In view of Paula's willful ignorance of the lease term, may Paula avoid the lease after she learns the term is five years? Did Paula know enough facts that she should have investigated before affirming instead of blundering ahead heedless of her ignorance? Under Restatement 91 & comment e, Paula may be found to have assumed the risk of proceeding with only generalized knowledge of the circumstances. Would it make any difference if the terms of similar farm leases customarily range between three and five years? One to two years? See Restatement §91 comment e, illustration 15.

Agency & Partnership
SPARK LAW SERIES

ANSWER:

A ratifier may elect to avoid an affirmance if at the time of the affirmance the ratifier was ignorant of any material fact involved in the affirm transaction. Restatement §91. Material facts are those which substantially affect the existence or extent of the obligations involved in the transaction, as distinguished from those which affect the values or inducements involved in the transaction. If the ratifier does not have actual knowledge of material facts, but only reason to know them, then the ratifier may avoid the affirmance.

PROBLEM 15.4: Expulsion

Levy, was a physician engaged in the practice of medicine as a partner in Nassau Queens Medical Group. By a majority vote of the partnership executive committee, Levy was expelled from the partnership on the ground that he was more than 70 yrs of age. The partnership agreement provided that a partner who was 70 yrs old or older could be terminated by a majority vote. Levy argues that the partners terminated him in bad faith. Other partners over the age of 70 were not expelled from the partnership. Levy believes that the real reason for the termination was Levy's criticisms of partnership decisions.

ANSWER:

UPA §38(1)

Dissolution and Liquidation – any assets of the partnership must be turned over to the partners in accordance w/ the partnership agreement. "The right given to each partner, where no agreement to the contrary has been made, to have his share of the surplus paid to him in cash makes certain an existing uncertainty." So expulsion of a partner who takes most of the assets can force dissolution of the partnership.

Agency & Partnership
SPARK LAW SERIES

Must make certain the expulsion does not trigger dissolution. The fiduciary duty remains even after expulsion although modified a bit. Dissolution agreements must have dissolution provisions that specify if expulsion can be done w/ or w/o cause.
- o The ONLY caveat of allowing for the agreement to state w/ or w/o cause, the Court <u>will require</u> that expulsion be for good cause and in good faith. (EX. firing your lawyer right before getting a big judgment – Ct will not allow it b/c it is in bad faith.)

<u>RUPA §601(3)</u> – allows expulsion pursuant to partnership agreement.

<u>RUPA §701</u> – uses the work "disassociate" to refer to expulsion.

HERE, the purpose of the termination clause (in the partnership agreement) was to provide a simple, practical and speedy method of separating a partner from the partnership, and in the absence of undue penalty or unjust forfeiture, the court may not frustrate this purpose. While <u>bad faith</u> may be actionable, there must be some showing that the partnership acted out of a desire to gain a business or property advantage for the remaining partners. Policy disagreements do not constitute bad faith since "at the heart of the partnership concept is the principle that partners may choose w/ whom they wish to be associated."

PROBLEM 15.5: *Dissociation of Owners from Firms*

[Judicial Expulsions / Owner Rights]

A general partnership for the operation of an insurance business was formed for a five-year term in 1934 with ten partners. Partner Brown held the majority interest in the business, with the other nine partners sharing the remainder. The partnership agreement provided that Brown would set the salaries of the partners, that the admission of a new partner would require the affirmative vote of a majority in

Agency & Partnership
SPARK LAW SERIES

number of the partners, and that all other decisions would be made by an affirmative vote of a majority in interest of the partnership. Brown proposed the admission of Moore as a new partner, but it was defeated by a 7-3 vote. Thereafter, Brown reduced the salaries of the seven plaintiffs by fifty percent. The seven plaintiffs sued for a dissolution of the partnership, and the trial court granted it. What decision on appeal? See Potter v. Brown

ANSWER:

UPA §32(1)(c) & (d): A partner's conduct is considered "wrongful" when it is taken in derogation of the duties imposed either explicitly by the partnership agreement or implicitly by virtue of the nature of the partnership itself. The UPA empowers a court to order partnership dissolution whenever, for example, a partner willfully or persistently commits a breach of the partnership or agreement, or otherwise so conducts himself in matters relating to the partnership business that it is not reasonably practicable to carry on the business in partnership with him.

There was a partnership agreement that a majority of a vote was needed. And Brown due to an unfavorable result decided to cut salaries. Because there was a decree of the court for dissolution based on the forgoing reasons, under §31(6) is reason for causes of dissolution.

UPA §32 – allows you to ask the Court for a Judicial Decree dissolving the partnership notwithstanding the partnership agreement.

RUPA §601(5) – On application by the partnership or another partner, the partner's expulsion by judicial determination b/c:
- the partner engaged in wrongful conduct that adversely and materially affected the partnership business;
- partner willfully or persistently committed a material breach of the partnership agreement or of a duty

owed to the partnership or the other partners under 404; OR
- <u>the partner engaged in conduct relating to the partnership business which makes it not reasonably practicable to carry on the business in partnership w/ the partner.</u>

<u>RUPA §801(1)</u> – Judicial expulsion DOES NOT dissolve the partnership (even in partnership at will).

<u>Default Rule</u> – Expulsion allows the other partners to leave (to dissolve the partnership) UNLESS the partnership agreement provides differently (then default rule doesn't apply).

PROBLEM 15.7: Dissociation of Owners from Firms

[Fiduciary Limits on Rights to Disassociation and Dissolution]

George and H.B. are partners in Santa Maria Linen Supply, which was formed in December, 1949, for the purpose of conducting a linen supply business in Santa Maria, California. The partners agreed that George would act as managing partner. During he first two years, each partner contributed approximately $43,000 to the partnership. The partners have no other written or oral agreements regarding the partnership or its affairs.

From 1949 to 1957, the partnership lost approximately $62,000. During 1958, Vandenberg Air Force Base opened nearby, and business began to improve. The partnership earned $3,824.41 in 1958 and $2,282.30 in the first three months of 1959. The partnership's chief obligations are $47,610.32 owed to Mission Supply Service on open account, and $12,794.21 owed to Bank of America.

Mission Supply Service, which is wholly owned by George, has sold the partnership all linen and machinery used in the day-to-day operation of its business form Mission Supply Service. Since 1949, the partnership has paid Mission Supply Service a total of $234,114.34.

Agency & Partnership
SPARK LAW SERIES

The proceeds of the loans from Bank of America was used to pay Mission Supply Service.

In April, 1959, George dissolved the partnership, and demanded that it be liquidated. H.B. argues that George is acting in bad faith, and is attempting to use his superior financial position to appropriate the now profitable business of the partnership. H.B. believes tat the amount owed Mission Supply Service may make it difficult to sell the business as a going concern. He fears that upon dissolution he will receive very little and that George will receive a business that has become very profitable because of the H.B. charges that George was content to share the losses but now that the business has become profitable, he wishes to keep all the gains. See Page v. Page,

ANSWER:

In insolvency law, we have principle of "bidding in" – meaning that creditor can play w/ the paper entity of the debtor. So if you're a creditor and you're owed $100 and an item is auctioned pursuant to dissolution, you can bid $100 but not go into your own pocket for that $100 item. You can simply refer to the claim and the $100 item. This is why in lots of business context; you find that the creditor ends up w/ the property.

There's probably enough evidence where this is over the line.

Failure to grant dissolution or ruling does not mean that the dissolution is unfair. As a consequence there will be a settlement between the parties.

NOTES

Looks like bad faith. Upon liquidation the partnership assets will be sold, who will they be sold to? George. Recall that in insolvency law, the principle of Bidding in plays a role. It means the creditor can manipulate the payment of ht debt. If you are cre4dirtoe or an items is auctions, you can bid 100, and you can refer to the claims, and still get the item. The creditor often ends up with the property. There is probably enough evidence that this is too much. So as a court you would try to fashion a more equitable solution. The court can do they by failing to grant that the dissolution is unfair. A settlement among the partners is more likely. This is an example of really Bad Faith. Bad Faith Dissolution as already discussed asks if this expulsion is the product of a plan to deny a partner what they have rightfully earned. You cannot take an action that is designed to benefit yourself as opposed to those you have a duty to.

Agency & Partnership
SPARK LAW SERIES

OUTLINE

Introduction to Firms

A. Introduction
   a. <u>Default rules</u>: rules which will govern the relationship of the parties absent specific agreement to the contrary
   b. <u>Full shield statute</u>: a statute which provides that there is no personal liability for debts of the partnership, regardless of how such debts are incurred
      i. Applies to LLP's in Texas
B. Types of Firms
   a. <u>Sole Proprietorships</u>: a business in which one person owns all the assets, owes all the liabilities, and operates in his or her personal capacity
   b. <u>Partnerships</u>: a partnership in which all partners participate fully in running the business and share equally in profits and losses, even though the partners' monetary contributions may vary
   c. <u>Limited Partnerships</u>: a partnership composed of one or more general partners and one or more limited partners
      i. <u>General partners</u>: partners who control the business and are personally liable for the partnership's debts
      ii. <u>Limited partners</u>: persons who contribute capital and share profits, but who cannot manage the business and are liable only for the amount of their contribution
   d. <u>Limited Liability Partnerships</u>: a partnership in which a partner is not liable for a negligent act committed by another partner or by an employee not under the partner's supervision
   e. <u>Limited Liability Limited Partnerships</u>: a limited partnership where the general partners have the same protections against personal liability that general partners do in an LLP possesses
   f. <u>Limited Liability Companies</u>: A company that is characterized by limited liability, management by members or managers, and limitations on ownership transfer
   g. Basic Characteristics of an LLC

Agency & Partnership
SPARK LAW SERIES

Entity Status	An LLC is an entity distinct from its members
Tax Treatment	An LLC is generally taxed as a partnership, unless its members elect to be taxed as a corporation
Profits and Losses	In most states, members share profits and losses of the LLC according to the value of their contributions
Management	An LLC may be managed by its members or managers
Liability of Members	A member is not liable for the LLC's obligations but is liable for her own torts
Transfer of Ownership	A member may assign her interest in the LLC but the assignment transfers only the member's right to receive distributions; management rights are not transferred.
Dissolution	An LLC will dissolve on the death, resignation, bankruptcy, incompetency, etc. of a member (unless the remaining members vote to continue the business)

      h. **Corporations**: An entity having authority under law to act as a single person distinct from the shareholders who own it and having the rights to issue stock and exist indefinitely
           i. C corporation: a corporation whose income is taxed through it rather than through its shareholders.
           ii. S corporation: a corporation whose income is taxed through its shareholders rather than through the corporation itself.
                1. Only corporations with a limited number of shareholders can elect S-corporation tax status
           iii. Any corporation not electing S-corporation tax status under the tax code is a C corporation by default

  C. The Firm and its Agents and Servants
      a. **Rest2d §1 Agency**: a fiduciary relationship resulting from...

Agency & Partnership
SPARK LAW SERIES

      i. One person (principal) making a manifestation of consent
          1. "Manifestation of Consent" is objective... it does not matter what the principal truly intended, rather the agency relationship depends on what the agent believed the principal intended. Thus, an agency relationship can arise even where the principal subjectively intended no such relationship.
      ii. That another person (agent) act on behalf of principal and
          1. What does this mean? An intermediary. Giving and receiving information. Power to bind a P to an agreement. Advise the P. Negotiate on behalf of P. A doesn't have to actual sign the contract.
      iii. Subject to principal's control
      iv. With consent by agent to do so.

b. **Rest2d §14J Agent or Buyer**: One who receives goods from another for resale to a third person is not thereby the other's agent in the transaction: whether he is an agent for this purpose or is himself a buyer depends upon whether the parties agree that his duty is to act *primarily* for the benefit of one delivering the goods to him or is to act *primarily* for his own benefit

c. **Factors in determining if there is an agency relationship:**
      i. A's power to alter P's legal relations
          1. What does this mean? A can bind P to a contract by executing instruments. Also, A can be authorized to transmit and receive information on behalf of P.
      ii. **A's fiduciary duty to act on behalf of P**
      iii. **P's right to control the A**
          1. How much control is needed?
              a. Master-Servant relationship: right to control the details of the work; physical conduct; manner of performance

     b. Principal-Agent relationship: principal sets task for agent; right to instruct
   2. What is the relationship between P-A and M-S? All masters are principals, all servants are agents.
   3. **Know the difference between M-S and P-A**
   4. When is someone a servant rather than an agent?? When the level of control is sufficiently high does a principal become a master and an agent a servant.
   5. A master is liable for servant's torts. A principal is not liable for agent's torts. A principal is liable for agent's contracts.
 d. **Rest2d §387 General Principle**: an agent has a duty to his principal to act solely for the benefit of the principal in all matters connected with his agency.
 e. The powers of the agent are to be exercised for the benefit of the principal only, and not of the agent or of third parties.
 f. An agent is under a strict duty to avoid any conflict between his or her self-interest and that of the principal.
 g. **Rest2d §389 Acting as Adverse Party Without Principal's Consent**: Unless otherwise agreed, an agent is subject to a duty not to deal with his principal as an adverse party in a transaction connected with his agency without the principal's knowledge.
   i. What does it mean to act as an adverse party? Self-dealing.
   ii. They cannot transact business with the principal without full disclosure.
 h. Where an agent breaches a duty to the principal and profits from the breach, the principal may maintain an action to recover those profits for himself.
 i. **Rest2d §388 Duty to Account for Profits Arising Out of Employment**: an agent who makes a profit in connection with transactions conducted by him on behalf of the principal is under a duty to give such profit to the principal.
 j. An agent's failure to disclose information material to the agency is a breach of the principal-agent relationship.

k. When legally sufficient evidence of an agency relationship is produced, the question of existence of the agency relationship is a factual matter and must be submitted to the jury.
l. **Rest2d §13 Agent as a Fiduciary, comment a:** *The Fiduciary Principle*: The agreement to act on behalf of the principal causes the agent to be a fiduciary, that is, a person having a duty, created by his undertaking, to act primarily for the benefit of another in matters connected with his undertaking.
    i. Among the agent's fiduciary duties to the principal is:
        1. The duty to account for profits arising out of the employment,
        2. The duty not to act as, or on account of, an adverse party without the principal's consent,
        3. The duty not to compete with the principal on his own account or for another in matters relating to the subject matter of the agency, and
        4. The duty to deal fairly with the principal in all transactions between them
m. **Rest2d §403 Liability for Things Received in Violation of Duty of Loyalty**: where an agent receives anything as a result of his violation of a duty of loyalty to the principal, he is subject to liability to deliver it, its value, or its proceeds, to the principal.
    i. The traditional equitable remedy against the agent is the constructive trust.
n. **Rest2d §407 Principal's Choice of Remedies**: if an agent has received a benefit as a result of violating his duty of loyalty, the principal is entitled to recover from him what he has so received, its value, or its proceeds, and also the amount of damage thereby caused.

Agency & Partnership
SPARK LAW SERIES

Duties of Principal and Agent

Duties	Remedies for Breach of Duties
Agent • Express contractual duties • Reasonable care in performance • Obedience • Notification • Loyalty	Principal • Contract remedies • Tort remedies • Action for secret profits • Rescission • Constructive trust • Accounting • Withhold compensation
Principal • Express contractual duties • Cooperation • Compensation • Reimbursement/indemnity • Avoidance of negligence	Agent • Contractual remedies • Indemnification • Possessory lien • Withholding further performance • Setoff • Accounting

D. The Firm and its Owners
    i. Entity vs. Aggregate Theories of Business Forms
        1. Aggregate vs. Entity: An entity is a separate and distinct thing from its owners. An aggregate is not separate and distinct from its owners.
            a. Entity: a legal person who is separate and distinct from the partners
            b. Aggregate: no separate legal person; only partners.
        2. Under UPA, partnerships are part aggregate and part entity
        3. Under RUPA, a partnership is an entity
    ii. Entity Defined
        1. UPA
            a. **UPA §6 Partnership Defined**: a partnership is an association of two or

more persons to carry on as co-owners of a business for profit.
i. *Comment*: the definition asserts that the associates are "co-owners" of the business. That distinguishes a partnership from an agency—an association of principal and agent. A business is a series of acts directed toward an end. Ownership involves the power of ultimate control. To state that partners are co-owners of a business is to state that they each have the power of ultimate control.
2. RUPA
a. **RUPA §201 Partnership as an Entity**: (a) a partnership is an entity distinct from its partners.
3. ULPA
a. **ULPA §2(1) Formation:** (1) Two or more persons desiring to form a limited partnership shall ...
4. RULPA
a. **RULPA §101(7) "Limited Partnership"**: a partnership formed by 2+ persons under the laws of this State and having 1+ general partners and 1+ limited partners.
5. Re-RULPA

iii. Nature of Partner's Liability
1. UPA
a. **UPA §15 Nature of Partner's Liability**: All partners are liable: (a) jointly and severally for everything chargeable to the partnership, (b) jointly for all others debts and obligations of the partnership; but any partner may enter into a separate obligation to perform a partnership contract.

2. RUPA
    a. **RUPA §306 Partner's Liability:**
        i. (a) All partners are liable jointly and severally for all obligations of the partnership unless otherwise agreed by the claimant or provided by law.
        ii. (b) A person admitted as a partner into an existing partnership is not personally liable for any partnership obligation incurred before the person's admission as a partner.
        iii. (c) An obligation of a partnership incurred while the partnership is a LLP, whether arising in contract, tort, or otherwise, is solely the obligation of the partnership. A partner is not personally liable, directly or indirectly, by way of contribution or otherwise, for such an obligation solely by reason of being or so acting as a partner.
3. RULPA
    a. **RULPA §403 General Powers and Liabilities:** (a) Except as provided in the act or the partnership agreement, a general partner of a limited partnership has the rights and powers and is subject to the restrictions of a partner in a partnership without limited partners. (b) Except as provided in the act, a general partner of a limited partnership has the liabilities of a partner in a partnership without limited partners to persons other than the partnership and the other partners. Except as provided in the act or the partnership agreement, a general partner of a limited partnership has the

liabilities of a partner in a partnership without limited partners to the partnership and to the other partners.
4. Re-RULPA
    a. **Re-RULPA §404 General Partner's Liability:**
        i. (a) Except as otherwise provided in (b) and (c), all general partners are liable jointly and severally for all obligations of the limited partnership unless otherwise agreed by the claimant or provided by law.
        ii. (b) A person that becomes a general partner of an existing limited partnership is not personally liable for an obligation of a limited partnership incurred before the person became a general partner.
        iii. (c) An obligation of a limited partnership incurred while the limited partnership is a limited liability limited partnership, whether arising in contract, tort, or otherwise, is solely the obligation of the limited partnership. A general partner is not personally liable, directly or indirectly, by way of contribution or otherwise, for such an obligation solely by reason of being or acting as a general partner. This applies despite anything inconsistent in the partnership agreement that existed immediately before the consent required to become a limited liability limited partnership.

iv. Rights and Duties of Partners
   1. UPA
      a. **UPA §18(e) Rules Determining Rights and Duties of Partners:** all partners have equal rights in the management and conduct of the partnership business.
   2. RUPA
      a. **RUPA §401(f) Partner's Rights and Duties:** each partner has equal rights in the management and conduct of the partnership business.
   3. ULPA
      a. **ULPA §9 Rights, Powers, and Liabilities of a General Partner:** (1) a general partner shall have all the rights and powers and be subject to all the restrictions and liabilities of a partner in a partnership without limited partners, except that without the written consent or ratification of the specific act by all the limited partners, a general partner or all of the general partners have no authority to
         i. Do any act in contravention of the certificate,
         ii. Do any act which would make it impossible to carry on the ordinary business of the partnership,
         iii. Confess a judgment against the partnership,
         iv. Possess or assign partnership property for a purpose other than for the partnership,
         v. Admit a person as a general partner,
         vi. Admit a person as a limited partner, unless the right to do so is in the certificate, or
         vii. Continue the business with partnership property on the

death, retirement or insanity of a general partner, unless the right to do so is given in the certificate.
  b. **ULPA §10 Rights of a Limited Partner**:
     i. (1) A limited partner shall have the same rights as a general partner to
        1. Have the partnership books kept at the principal place of business of the partnership, and at all times to inspect and copy any of them.
        2. Have on demand true and full information of all things affecting the partnership, and a formal account of partnership affairs whenever circumstances render it just and reasonable, and
        3. Have dissolution and winding up by decree of court
     ii. (2) A limited partner shall have the right to receive a share of the profits or other compensation by way of income and to the return of his contribution.
     iii. Notice no power to control.

Agency & Partnership
SPARK LAW SERIES

SUMMARY OF RIGHTS OF PARTNERS

Management	All partners have an equal right to participate in the management of the partnership unless the partnership agreement provides otherwise.
Inspection	A partner has a right to inspect and copy the partnership books and records
Distributions	Partners have whatever rights are granted in the partnership agreement as to distributions of profits. If the agreement is silent, partner's share profits equally; upon dissolution, partners have the right to the return of their capital contributions
Indemnification	A partner has a right to be indemnified by fellow partners for expenses and personal liabilities incurred on behalf of the partnership.
Remuneration	Partners generally have no right to remuneration for their services to the partnership except for winding up the partnership business.

RIGHTS OF A LIMITED PARTNER

- → Share in partnership profits and losses and receive distributions
- → Transact business with the partnership
- → Assign her interest
- → Withdraw from the partnership
- → Bring a derivative action
- → Inspect and copy partnership records and obtain from a general partner information concerning the state and financial condition of the partnership
- → Vote on limited issues

v. Liability to Third Parties
   1. RULPA
      a. **RULPA §303(a) Liability to Third Parties:** Except as provided in (d), a limited partner is not liable for the obligations of a limited partnership unless he is also a general partner or, in addition to the exercise of his rights and powers as a limited partner, he participates in the control of the business. However, if the limited partner participates in the control of the business, he is liable only to persons who transact business with the limited partnership reasonably believing, based upon the limited partner's conduct, that the limited partner is a general partner.

Agency & Partnership
SPARK LAW SERIES

LIABILITY OF A LIMITED PARTNER TO THIRD PARTIES

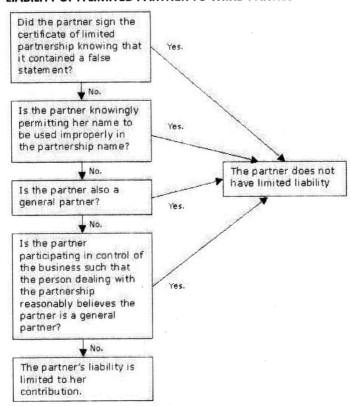

COMPARISON OF A PARTNER'S LIABILITY TO 3RD PERSONS

	UPA	RUPA	RUPA-LLP
Liability for contracts	Joint	Joint and Several	Not Liable
Liability for Torts	Joint and Several	Joint and Several	Not liable except for own misconduct
Liability for Co-Partner's Crimes	Not Liable	Not Liable	Not Liable

b. Limited Liability Companies
   i. ULLCA
      1. **ULLCA §101(12) Member-managed company**: an LLC other than a manager-managed company.
         a. Default Rule
      2. **ULLCA §101(11) Manager-managed company**: an LLC which is so designated in its articles of organization.
         a. You have to designate yourself this way or else you're member-managed
      3. **ULLCA §101(13) operating agreement**: the agreement under §103 concerning the relations among the members, managers, and LLC. The term includes amendments to the agreement.
      4. **ULLCA §103(a) Effect of Operating Agreement**: Except for (b), all members of a LLC may enter into an operating agreement, <u>which need not be in writing</u>, to regulate the affairs of the company and the conduct of its business, and to govern relations among the members, managers, and company. To the extent the operating agreement does not otherwise provide, the act governs relations among the members, managers, and company.
      5. **ULLCA §201 Limited Liability Company as Legal Entity**: A limited liability company is a legal entity distinct from its members.
      6. **ULLCA §404(a) and (b) Management of Limited Liability Company**:
         a. (a) In a *member-managed company*, each member has equal rights in the management and conduct of the company's business, and any matter relating to the business of the company may be decided by a majority of the members.

b. (b) In a *manager-managed company*, each manager has equal rights in the management and conduct of the company's business; any matter relating to the business of the company may be exclusively decided by the manager or, if there is more than one manager, by a majority of the manager, and a manager must be designated, appointed, elected, removed, or replaced by a vote, approval, or consent of a majority of the members, and holds office until a successor has been elected and qualified, unless the manager sooner resigns or is removed.

ii. What is a derivative suit? A suit brought by owners (members) on behalf of the company (the cause of action belongs to the LLC).

iii. What's the difference between the <u>affairs</u> of the LLC and the <u>conduct</u> of the business? The conduct of the business is how the business is going to be run. The affairs of the LLC how things are going to be handled.

Agency & Partnership
SPARK LAW SERIES

LIABILITY OF PRINCIPAL FOR AGENT'S TORTS

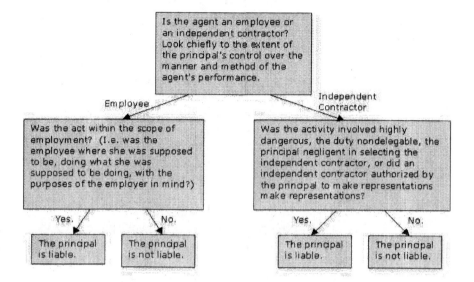

Contractual Dealings by Agents

    A. Firm's Liability in Contract for Acts of its Agents
        a. A principal is liable for the authorized acts of agents.
        b. Hypo: P authorized A to contract for the purchase of a car. A goes third party and signs a K obligating P to buy the car. Then there's a problem... say the P really only authorized the purchase of a Toyota Prius, and the agent bought was a Ford F-150.
            i. Is principal liable on the contract? No.
            ii. Would the P be liable to the Toyota dealer to buy a Prius too? No. Rest2d §164(1).
            iii. Say the instructions to A were to buy a Prius for no more than $25K. So the A pays $28K for a Prius. Is P liable for the other $3K? No.
            iv. If Dealer would be willing to sell the car for $25K, is P liable on the K? Yes, per the general rule's exception.
        c. **General Rule**: if there is any variation from what authority A's given, the P is not liable.

i. **Exception**: If the only variation is to amount, the third party can choose to go with the amount of authorized, and P will be liable. This also applies to separable parts.
d. An agency relationship is either actual or ostensible.
i. It's <u>actual</u> when the principal appoints the agent
ii. It's <u>ostensible</u> when the principal by conduct or want of ordinary care causes a third person to believe another, who is not actually appointed, to be his agent. An ostensible agency must be traceable to the principle and cannot be established solely by the acts, declarations, or conduct of the agent.
e. When an agent exceeds his authority, his principal is bound by his authorized acts so far only as they can be plainly separated from those which are unauthorized.
f. **Rest2d §7 Authority**: authority is the agent's power to bind the principal by acts done in accordance with the principal's manifestations of consent to the agent.
g. **Rest2d §159 Apparent Authority**: A principal is bound by the authorized acts of his or her agent in entering into contracts on the principal's behalf.
h. **Rest2d §8B Estoppel**: Under certain circumstances, agents may have power to bind the principal by unauthorized acts, such as where the agent has apparent authority or inherent agency power, or where the principal is estopped from denying the agent's authority.
i. **Rest2d §164(1) Contracts Unauthorized in Part**: where an agent enters into an unauthorized contract without having the power to bind the principal, the principal is not bound by the contract as actually made by the agent, or as it would have been made if the agent had acted within his or her authority.
j. **Rest2d §151 Sealed Instruments & §152 Negotiable Instruments**: At common law, a principal is not bound by the authorized contracts of his or her agent where the contract is under seal or is a negotiable instrument.
k. **Rest2d §21 Capacity of Agent in General**: to be an agent, a person needs only the physical or mental capabilities to do the thing he has been appointed to do.
B. Firm's Rights Under Contracts Entered into by its Agents

Agency & Partnership
SPARK LAW SERIES

a. Third persons dealing with an agent may not know they are dealing with an agent,
   i. <u>Undisclosed Principal</u>: where the 3rd person has no notice that the agent is acting for a principal
   ii. <u>Partially Disclosed Principal</u>: where 3rd person knows their dealing with an agent, but they do not know the identity of the principal
   iii. <u>Disclosed Principal</u>: where the 3rd person has notice both that the agent is acting for a principal and knows the identity of the principal
b. Can an undisclosed P enforce the K made between the 3rd party and A?
   i. CL agency = a 3rd party to a K can sue the undisclosed P (so the converse must be true)
      1. Undisclosed P is liable on the K, and is a party to the K, even though their name is not in the K.
      2. Trouble is that how can you let a person enforce a K when their name is not on the K? Risk of double liability. Resolution is to have a prudent third party to check with the A before delivering to the P; and *res judicata*.
   ii. A entered into a K with the 3rd party on behalf of P, so P is liable; therefore, P ought to be able to enforce the K as well.
c. **Rest2d §302 General Rule**: A person who makes a contract with an agent of an undisclosed principal, intended by the agent to be on account of his principal and within the power of such to bind his principal, is liable to the principal as if the principal himself had made the contract with him, unless he is excluded by the form or terms of the contract, unless his existence is fraudulently concealed or unless there is a set-off or similar defense against the agent.
d. **Prête-nom**: ("name lending") The agent was lending their name to the principal when the K was made. Under the doctrine of *prête-nom*, undisclosed principals are not parties to contracts entered into by their *prête-noms*. Only the *prête-nom* may sue or be sued on such contracts; the principals may not sue or be sued in their own names.

e. **General Rule:** the principal can be bound on a contract that was not specifically made on behalf of the principal
   i. **Exceptions:**
      1. **Rest2d §304 Agent Misrepresents Existence of Principal**: A person with whom an agent contracts on account of an undisclosed principal can rescind the K if he was induced to enter into it by a representation that the agent was not acting for a principal and if, as the agent or principal has notice, he would not have dealt with the principal.
      2. **Rest2d §303, comment c, Principal Excluded from Transaction, non assignment clause**: A clause in the K against assignment does not of itself prevent the principal from bringing suit upon the K. The existence of such a clause, however, may be considered as evidence that the parties intended to exclude the principal or that failure to reveal the existence of a principal is fraudulent within the rule stated in §304 if there is other evidence to that effect.
      3. **Rest2d §306 Rights between other party and agent: (1)** If the agent has been authorized to conceal the existence of the principal, the liability to an undisclosed principal of a person dealing with an agent within his power to bind the principal is diminished by any claim which such person may have against the agent at the time of making the contract and until the existence of the principal becomes known to him, if he could set off such claim in an action against the agent. **(2)** If the agent is authorized only to contract in the principal's name, the other party does not have set-off for a claim due him from the agent unless the agent has been entrusted with the possession of chattels which he dispose of as directed or unless the

principal has otherwise misled the third person into extending credit to the agent.
C. Agent's Liability for Contractual Dealings
   a. Agent's duty to Fully Disclose Principal
      i. A P is always liable on K made by A's within the scope of authority and power.
      ii. Members of an LLC are never personally liable as members, but if they deal as individuals then they could be liable.
      iii. The agent has a duty to fully disclose the fact of the agency and the ID of the P if he does not want to be liable on an obligation. This even applies if it is partially disclosed. Under this rule for disclosure, the A and P are alternatively liable, have to make an election of remedies and decide which one to sue.
      iv. Disclosing the business name of the company (like just handing over a business card) is not enough to adequately disclose the P.
      v. A third party can be put on notice of the agency relationship and the ID of the P if they actually know, should know, or have reason to know.
      vi. **Rest2d §4 partially disclosed principal**: a principal is at least partially disclosed where the third person has notice the agent is acting for a principal, and fully disclosed where the third person also has notice of the identity of the principal.
         1. Persons have notice of a fact when they know it, have reason to know it, or should have known it.
      vii. **Rest2d §321 Principal partially disclosed**: Unless otherwise agreed, an agent acting for a partially disclosed principal is a party to a contract entered into on behalf of the principal
      viii. **Rest2d §321, comment a**: The inference of an understanding that the agent is a party to the contract exists unless the agent gives such complete information concerning his principal's identity that he can be readily distinguished. If the party has no reasonable means of ascertaining the principal, the inference is almost irresistible and prevails in the absence of an agreement to the contrary.

b. Agent's Implied Warranty of Authority
   i. If the agent purports to act on behalf of a principal, but has no authority, then he has breached an implied warranty of authority. The A may be sued under that breach but not under the K b/c he is not a party to the K.
   ii. Hypo: P does not authorize A to act a certain way, and A goes ahead and acts anyway – A is making an implied warranty of authority (there is not express warranty). This does not depend on a K either; this warranty arises from the relationship. A breach of the implied warranty of authority is a tort, not a K claim. One who purports to act as another's agent but has no authority is personally liable on the implied warranty of authority to the one who deals in GF reliance thereon.
   iii. Death terminates an agency
   iv. A warranty is a guarantee – a guarantee that A has authority and the P is alive. To not be personally liable if the P dies, maybe disclaim it.
   v. Another way for the A to be liable, commit a tort on instructions from P b/c that is joint and several liability.
   vi. **Rest2d §329, comment k, Agent who warrants authority; when a cause of action arises**: a cause of action against an agent for a breach of his implied warranty of authority accrues when the third person learns that the agent does not have authority, or when he suffers damage or fails to gain the anticipated benefits, whichever occurs first.
   vii. **Rest2d §329, comment f, Agent who warrants authority; where principal is bound**: If the principal becomes a party to the transaction, the rights of the other party are not affected by the fact that the agent committed a wrong to his principal.

Agency & Partnership
SPARK LAW SERIES

AGENT'S LIABILITY TO THIRD PARTY WHEN ACTING WITHOUT AUTHORITY

	For Breach of Warranty	On Contract
Disclosed Principal Situation	Agent Liable	Agent NOT Liable
Partially Disclosed Principal Situation	Agent Liable	Agent Liable
Undisclosed Principal Situation	Agent NOT Liable	Agent Liable

SUMMARY OF CONTRACT LIABILITY TO THIRD PARTIES

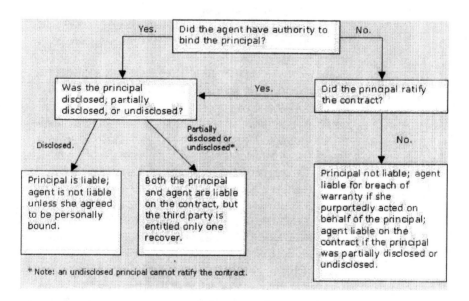

*Note: an undisclosed principal cannot ratify the contract.

Formation of Firms

A. Agency Relationships
   a. If you don't follow the statute that creates the agency relationship then you have a defective agency relationship.
   b. **Rest2d § 26 Creation Of Authority; General Rule:** Except for the execution of instruments under seal or for the performance of transactions required by statute to be

authorized in a particular way, authority to do an act can be created by written or spoken words or other conduct of the principal which, reasonably interpreted, causes the agent to believe that the principal desires him so to act on the principal's account.
  c. <u>Equal Dignity Rule</u>: (statutory): if you want the agent to do something that requires certain formalities, and you want an agent to act on your behalf, the appointing of the agent must meet the same formalities of the thing you want him to do. I.e.: Whatever the level of formalities required for the underlying document are required for the appointing of agent.
      i. Common law is opposite—no formalities needed for appointing an agent.
      ii. Texas says that no writing is required. I.e. Equal dignity not required at common law and in Texas, only in a limited context (deeds).
  d. Agent would be liable to principal only if he breached duty to act with reasonable care and skill
  e. **Rest2d §377**: one who makes a contract with another to perform services as an agent for him is subject to a duty to act according to his promise.
      i. Comment b says that under ordinary circumstances, the promise to act as an agent is interpreted as being a promise only to make reasonable efforts to accomplish the directed results. If so interpreted, the promisor is not liable unless he fails to make such efforts as he reasonably can.
  f. Agency is both contractual and fiduciary.
  g. **Rest2d §15**: An agency relation exists only if there has been a manifestation by the principal to the agent that the agent may act on the principal's account and consent by the agent so to act.
  h. **Rest2d §16**: Unlike traditional contracts, creation of the agency relationship does not require a mutual exchange of consideration.
  i. **Rest2d §376**: The nature and extent of the duties to which any particular fiduciary is subject are determined by the terms of the agreement between the parties and interpreted in light of the circumstances

Agency & Partnership
SPARK LAW SERIES

j. **Rest2d §400**: an agent who commits a breach of his contract with his principal is subject to liability to the principal in accordance with the principles of the Rest of Contracts.
   i. Comment a says that the application of the rules which apply to contracts in general is sometimes unique when applied to agency situations, but there is no inconsistency between the rule of the two subjects.

B. Partnerships
   a. UPA
      i. **UPA §7 Rules for Determining the Existence of a Partnership**: In determining whether a partnership exists, these rules shall apply:
         1. Persons who are not partners as to each other are not partners as to third persons
         2. Joint tenancy, tenancy in common, tenancy by the entireties, joint property, common property, or part ownership does not of itself establish a partnership, whether such co-owners do or do not share any profits made by the use of the property
            a. Does this make sense? Doesn't owning property together mean there's a partnership?
         3. The sharing of gross returns does not of itself establish a partnership, whether or not the person sharing them have a joint or common right or interest in any property from which the returns are derived.
         4. The receipt by a person of a share of the profits of a business is prima facie evidence that he is a partner in the business, but no such inference shall be drawn if such profits were received in payment:
            a. As a debt by installments or otherwise
            b. As wages of an employee or rent to a landlord
            c. As an annuity to a widow or representative of a deceased partner

Agency & Partnership
SPARK LAW SERIES

        d. As interest on a loan, though the amount of payment vary with the profits of the business,
        e. As the consideration for the sale of a goodwill of a business or other property by installments or otherwise.
    ii. **UPA §18(a) Rules Determining Rights and Duties of Partners**: The right and duties of the partners in relation to the partnership shall be determined, subject to any agreement between them, by the following rules: (a) each partner shall be repaid his contributions, whether by way of capital or advances to the partnership property and share equally in the profits and surplus remaining after all liabilities, including those to partners, are satisfied; and must contribute towards the losses, whether of capital or otherwise, sustained by the partnership according to his share in the profits.

b. RUPA
    i. **RUPA §202(a) Formation of a Partnership**: The association of 2+ persons to carry on as co-owners a business for profit forms a partnership, whether or not the persons intend to form a partnership.
    ii. **RUPA §401(a)(2) Partner's Rights and Duties**: Each partner is deemed to have an account that is charged with an amount equal to the money plus the value of any other property, net of the amount of any liabilities, distributed by the partnership to the partner and the partner's share of the partnership losses.

c. **Factors courts look at to determine if people acting enough as partners to be considered partners**
    i. If they're co owners
    ii. If they share profits
    iii. If they exert control/management
    iv. What kind of contribution was put in.
    v. Intent
    vi. Conduct (agreed to and what was actually done)

d. Traditional rule is that partners cannot sue each other or the partnership for matters arising out of partnership affairs – but

Agency & Partnership
SPARK LAW SERIES

RUPA §405 now allows suits by a partner against another partner for claims arising out of the partnership affairs, etc.
- e. **Must look to (1) the written agreement or (2) the conduct...to determine if it was a partnership**
    - i. (Need all 4 elements of intent; business; profit; co-ownership of profits, property and control).
    - ii. Conduct = question of fact. Still neither party by their conduct intended to form a partnership relationship. They still had a business. It was for profit. And, by conduct, there was still no co-ownership of anything.
- f. UPA §7(4), RUPA §202(c)(3) - persons who share profits are presumed to be partners, unless they are being received in a non-partnership capacity (wages, rent, etc.).
- g. <u>Joint Venture</u>: a business undertaking by two or more parties in which the profits, losses and control are shared
    - i. It's similar to a partnership
    - ii. Joint venture vs. Partnership:
        1. A joint venture is formed for the purpose of carrying on a single transaction or project, rather than a series (which would be a business).
        2. A joint venture is kinda partnership, but to carry on a single transaction, not a continuing business. Sometimes a single project is not a business and technically not a partnership.
        3. Even though a joint venture is not a partnership, courts often apply partnership law, including the UPA to them
    - iii. **Common law test for joint ventures:**
        1. **A community of interest**
        2. **An agreement to share profits as principals**
        3. **An agreement to share losses, costs, and expenses, and**
        4. **Mutual rights of control**
    - iv. Texas SCt said: In joint ventures, unless there is an express agreement to share losses, the court will not make them share the loss
        1. Same result today? No. TRPA 2.03(c).

Agency & Partnership
SPARK LAW SERIES

SUMMARY OF FACTORS INDICATING A PARTNERSHIP

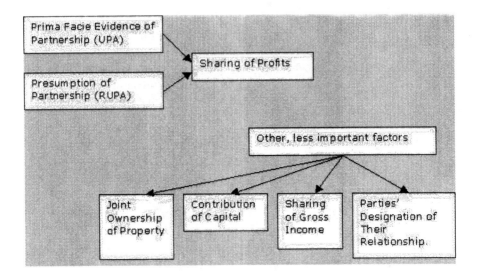

- C. Firms with Limited Liability
    - a. ULPA
        - i. **ULPA §1: Limited Partnership Defined**: a limited partnership is a partnership formed by 2+ persons having as members one or more general partners and one or more limited partners. The limited partners as such shall not be bound by the obligations of the partnership.
        - ii. **ULPA §17(1) Liability of Limited Partner to Partnership**: a limited partner is liable to the partnership (a) for the difference between his contribution as actually made and that stated in the certificate as having been made, and (b) for any unpaid contribution which he agreed in the certificate to make in the future at the time and on the conditions stated in the certificate.
        - iii. **ULPA §2(2) Formation**: a limited partnership is formed if there has been substantial compliance in good faith with the requirements.
    - b. ULLCA
        - i. **ULLCA §105(a) Name**: The name of an LLC must contain: Limited liability company or limited

Agency & Partnership
SPARK LAW SERIES

        company OR L.L.C. or LLC or L.C. or LC. Limited can be abbreviated Ltd. Company can be abbreviated Co.

  ii. **ULLCA §108 Designated Office and Agent for Service**: A LLC shall designate and continuously maintain in the state an office and an agent.

  iii. **ULLCA §112 Nature of Business and Powers**: Unless otherwise agreed, an LLC has the same powers as an individual to do all things necessary or convenient to carry on its business affairs, including power to
1. Sue and be sued,
2. Purchase, receive, lease, etc property,
3. Sell, convey, mortgage all or any part of its property,
4. Purchase, receive, etc shares or other interests in or obligations of any other entity,
5. Make K's,
6. Lend money,
7. Be a promoter, partner, member, associate, or manager of any partnership,
8. Conduct its business,
9. Elect managers and appoint officers,
10. Pay pensions,
11. Make donations for the public welfare, and
12. Make payments or donations that further the business of the LLC.

  iv. **ULLCA §202 Organization**: One or more persons may organize an LLC. Unless a delayed effective date is specified, the existence of a LLC begins when the articles of organization are filed. The filing of the articles of organization by the Sec of State is conclusive proof that the organizers satisfied all conditions precedent to the creation of an LLC.

  v. **ULLCA §204 Amendment or restatement of articles of organization**: The articles of amendment must set forth the: (1) name of the LLC; (2) date of filing of the articles of organization; and (3) amendment to the articles. A LLC may restate its articles of organization at any time.

Agency & Partnership
SPARK LAW SERIES

- vi. **ULLCA §208 Certificate of existence or authorization:** (d) Subject to any qualification stated in the certificate, a certificate of existence or authorization issued by the Sec of State may be relied upon as conclusive evidence that the domestic or foreign LLC is in existence or is authorized to transact business in this State.
- vii. **ULLCA §209 Liability for false statement in filed record:** If a record authorized or required to be filed under this Act contains a false statement, one who suffers loss by reliance on the statement may recover damages for the loss from a person who signed the record or caused another to sign it on the person's behalf and knew the statement to be false at the time the record was signed.
- viii. **ULLCA §210 Filing by judicial act:** If a person required by §205 to sign any record fails or refuses to do so, any other person who is adversely affected by the failure or refusal may petition the appropriate court to direct the signing of the record. If the court finds that it is proper for the record to be signed and that a person so designated has failed or refused to sign the record, it shall order the Sec of State to sign and file an appropriate record.

c. Delaware
   i. Delaware LLC § 18-101 Definitions
   ii. Delaware LLC § 18-102 Name set forth in certificate
   iii. Delaware LLC § 18-104 Registered office; registered agent:
   iv. Delaware LLC § 18-106 Nature of business permitted; powers:
   v. Delaware LLC § 18-201 Certificate of formation.
   vi. Delaware LLC § 18-203 Cancellation of certificate:
   vii. Delaware LLC § 18-207 Notice:

d. Contracts entered into before formation of a limited liability firm
   i. HYPO: Grace, Alice, and Lewis were going to create an LLC under name White Rabbit Records. At the time of the transaction in question, they were not

yet an LLC. Grace signed a lease under WWR's name. Alice signed with an artist. All these were done before the Certificate of Organization was issued.
   1. Is the LLC liable under the lease? No, they had not adopted the contract either expressly or impliedly. Why? Because they were not in existence when the contract was made.
   2. Is Grace liable to landlord? Yes, because
       a. she acted on behalf of a principal that did not exist.
       b. Implied warranty of authority
       c. She didn't fully disclose she was an agent of an identified principal
   3. Is Alice liable to artist? Yes, because she acted as agent to artist.
   4. Is there anyway to get her out of liability? Get the LLC formed and get the LLC to adopt the agreement.
   5. What wrinkle does *Dwinell v. Cosmo Hotel* bring in? The substantial compliance defense. Does this theory make Lewis liable? There was no LL formed, so by default, it was a general partnership. Why is it a general partnership instead of anything else? Because it's the only partnership that exists at common law (read: without statute).

ii. Traditional approach
   1. Promoter Liability (a.k.a. Pre-formation contracts)
       a. This is where there is liability of agents who contract on behalf of the entity-to-be.
       b. <u>Promoter</u>: anyone who undertakes to form a corporation and to procure for it the rights, instrumentalities, and capital by which it is to carry out the purpose set forth in its charter

c. <u>Novation</u>: the act of substituting for an old obligation a new one that either replaces an existing obligation with a new one or replaces an original party with a new one.
d. Where a promoter wishes to be released from liability for contracts he makes on behalf of a corporation not yet formed, he has the burden of proving the existence of an agreement to release him. The mere facts of contracting in the corporate name and payments made to the corporation are not sufficient to carry that burden.
e. The legal relationship between a promoter and the corporate enterprise he seeks to advance is analogous to that between an agent and his principal... so the legal principles are the same.
f. Promoters are released from liability only where the contract provides that performance is to be the obligation of the corporation, the corporation is ultimately formed, and the corporation then formally adopts the contract.
g. Mere adoption of the contract by the corporation will not relieve promoters from liability in the absence of a subsequent novation.
h. **Rest2d §326**: Unless otherwise agreed, a person who, in dealing with another, purports to act as agent for a principal whom both know to be nonexistent or wholly incompetent, becomes a party to such a contract.

                i. The actual intent of the parties is a question of fact
            2. In corporation cases, the corporate principal is deemed not to exist until it has complied with the formalities required by state law for the formation of a corporation. The same reasoning should apply to dealings on behalf of an LP, LLP, or a LL that is in the process of being formed.
            3. While courts are lax as to the literal requirements of the formation of partnership statutes, the statutes does contemplate at least <u>substantial compliance</u> with the requirements.
            4. Texas courts require strict compliance with the statutes to create an entity.
            5. Common Law Approach (Pre-UPLA): persons who believe they are limited partners, but who are not because no limited partnership certificate was ever filed.
                a. Called a defective limited partnership
        iii. ULPA
            1. **ULPA §11 Status of Person Erroneously Believing Himself a Limited Partner**: A person who has contributed to the capital of a business conducted by a person or partnership erroneously believing that he has become a limited partner in a limited partnership, is not, by reason of his exercise of the rights of a limited partner, a general partner with the person or in the partnership carrying on the business, or bound by the obligations of such person or partnership.
        iv. RULPA
            1. **RULPA §207(1) Liability for False Statement in Certificate:** If any certificate of limited partnership or certificate of amendment contains a false statement, one who suffers

loss by reliance on the statement may recover damages for the loss from (i) any person who executes (or causes to be executed) and knew about the falsity, and (ii) any GP who knew or should have known the statement to be false at the time of execution.

2. **RULPA §304 Person Erroneously Believing Himself an Limited Partner:**
    a. Except as provided in §b, a person who makes a contribution to a business enterprise and erroneously but in good faith believes that he has become a limited partner in the enterprise is not a GP and is not bound by its obligations by reason of making the contribution, or receiving distributions from the enterprise, or exercising any right of an limited partner if, upon finding out about the mistake he (1) causes an appropriate certificate of limited partnership (or amendment) to be executed and filed, OR (2) withdraws from future equity participation in the enterprise by filing a certificate of withdrawal with the Sec of State.
    b. A person who makes a contribution described in §a is liable as a GP to any 3rd party who transacts business with the enterprise (i) before the person withdraws and an appropriate certificate is filed to show withdrawal, or (ii) before an appropriate certificate is filed to show that he is not a GP, but in either case only if the 3rd party actually believed in good faith that

the person was a GP at the time of the transaction.
3. **RULPA §502 Liability for Contribution:** (a) A promise by a limited partner to contribute is not enforceable unless in a signed writing. (b) Except as provided in the partnership agreement, a partner is obligated to the limited partnership to perform any enforceable promise to contribute cash, property, or services. If they don't, he is obligated at the option of the limited partnership to contribute cash equal in value. (c) Unless otherwise provided in the partnership agreement, the obligation of a partner to make a contribution or return money or other property paid or distributed in violation of RULPA may be compromised only by consent of all the partners. Notwithstanding the compromise, a creditor of a limited partner who extends credit or otherwise acts in reliance on that obligation after the partner signs a writing that reflects the obligation and before the amendment or cancellation thereof to reflect the compromise may enforce the original obligation.

v. Re-RULPA
  1. **Re-RULPA §306 Person Erroneously Believing Self to be Limited Partner:**
      a. Except as otherwise provided in subsection (b), a person that makes an investment in a business enterprise and erroneously but in good faith believes that the person has become a limited partner in the enterprise is not liable for the enterprise's obligations by reason of making the investment, receiving distributions from the enterprise, or exercising any rights of or appropriate to a limited

partner, if, on ascertaining the mistake, the person: (1) causes an appropriate certificate of limited partnership, amendment, or statement of correction to be signed and delivered to the Sec of State for filing; or (2) withdraws from future participation as an owner in the enterprise by signing and delivering to the Sec of State for filing a statement of withdrawal under this section.

b. A person that makes an investment described in subsection (a) is liable to the same extent as a general partner to any third party that enters into a transaction with the enterprise, believing in good faith that the person is a general partner, before the Sec of State files a statement of withdrawal, certificate of limited partnership, amendment, or statement of correction to show that the person is not a general partner.

c. If a person makes a diligent effort in good faith to comply with subsection (a)(1) and is unable to cause the appropriate certificate of limited partnership, amendment, or statement of correction to be signed and delivered to the Sec of State for filing, the person has the right to withdraw from the enterprise pursuant to subsection (a)(2) even if the withdrawal would otherwise breach an agreement with others that are or have agreed to become co-owners of the enterprise.

Agency & Partnership
SPARK LAW SERIES

- i. §(b) limits §(a) by allowing a third party who had transacted business with the "LP" prior to the curative act (filing or withdrawing) to hold would-be limited partners liable as general partners if the third party actually believed in good faith that person where general partners.

vi. A person is liable as a limited partner with respect to third parties dealing with the enterprise, even though they really are general partners when:
   1. There is a good faith belief at the time of the contribution that they were limited partners and
   2. A proper certificate was filed or notice of withdrawal was given. (This is from RULPA §304(a)) Satisfaction of §304(a) effectively cuts off all personal liability as a general partner, unless (b) applies. (See above)

vii. At common law, corporations could be either
   1. <u>De jure corporation</u>: a corporation which has been created as a result of the compliance with all of the constitutional or statutory requirements of a particular governmental entity
      a. Think of it as a corporation at law
   2. <u>De facto corporation</u>: a corporation that can be brought into being when it can be shown that a bona fide and colorable attempt has been made to create a corporation, even though the efforts at incorporation can be shown to be irregular, informal or even defective.
      a. Think of it as a corporation in fact
      b. *Focus on*: What are the elements? What does it mean to say a

corporation is de facto? Is the de facto doctrine equitable?
- c. **Elements of De facto Corporation**
  - i. A valid law existed under which such a corporation could be lawfully organized
  - ii. An attempt had been made to organize thereunder
  - iii. The defective corporation was an actual user of the corporate franchise
  - iv. Good faith in claiming to be and in doing business as a corporation
  - v. Third party dealt with them as if they were a limited liability entity, not as a principal

3. <u>Corporation by estoppel</u>: a corporation that comes about when the parties thereto are estopped from denying a corporate existence. The parties may, by their agreement or conduct, estop themselves from denying the existence of the corporation
   - a. **Elements of Corporation by Estoppel:**
     - i. Misleading conduct by the person to be estopped
     - ii. Causing third party reason to believe it
     - iii. Third part changes positions to their detriment

viii. All persons who assume to act as a limited liability company without authority to do so shall be jointly and severally liable for all debts and liabilities

Agency & Partnership
SPARK LAW SERIES

ix. A limited liability company shall not transact business or incur indebtedness, except that which is incidental to its organization or to obtaining subscriptions for or payment of contributions, until the articles of organization have been filed by the Dept of State

x. A promoter of an LLC must take steps to create a new company. The very nature of a legal entity created by a formal filing with the state requires that certain actions be taken prior to incorporation.

WILL AGENT'S ACTS BIND THE PRINCIPAL?

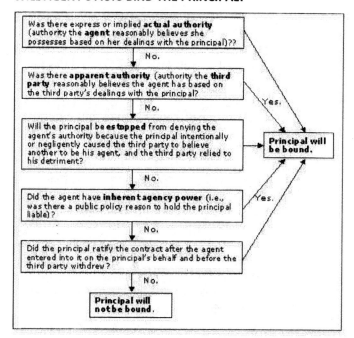

Agency & Partnership
SPARK LAW SERIES

Actual Authority of Agents and its consequences

A. **Actual Authority**: actual authority arises from the manifestation of consent from the principal to the agent (not to a third person) that the agent should act for the principal. It includes the power to do whatever the principal has engaged the agent to accomplish and is controlled by the agent's reasonable beliefs (i.e. the agent has actual authority to act in any manner that a reasonable person in the agent's position would believe was authorized by the principal's words or conduct.
   a. Two types of actual authority: (1) express authority, (2) implied authority
   b. Actual authority is either expressed or implied.
      i. If authority is not expressed, it's implied.
      ii. Implied authority can be implied-in-fact or implied-in-law
   c. Apparent authority vs. Actual authority
      i. <u>Apparent authority</u>: authority that a third party reasonably believes an agent has, based on the third party's dealing with the principal
      ii. <u>Actual authority</u>: authority that a principal intentionally confers on an agent, including the authority that the agent reasonably believes he or she has as a result of the agent's dealings with the principal
      iii. Only actual authority can be expressly conferred upon an agent.
      iv. The other kinds of authority—inherent and apparent/estoppel—necessarily arise by implication.
      v. Inherent authority is implied in law.

B. <u>Express Actual Authority</u>: authority expressly granted; actual authority contained within the four corners of the agency agreement between the principal and the agent

   a. <u>Power of attorney</u>: a written instrument conferring authority on an agent
   b. <u>Special Power of Attorney</u>: power of attorney to do certain acts only

- c. <u>General Power of Attorney</u>: power of attorney to transact all business for the principal
- d. Any vagueness or uncertainty as to the scope of a power of attorney is normally construed against the principal
- e. Powers of attorney are interpreted narrowly
- f. Gifts are not to be conferred unless express and unambiguous
- g. Things that are too personal are not allowed to be authorized under a power of attorney
    - i. Health care decisions (pulling plug or not)
        1. Statutes provide for a health care power of attorney just for this type of thing
    - ii. Divorces
- h. An agent holding a broad power of attorney lacks the power to make a gift of the principal's property unless that power (1) is expressly conferred, (2) arises as a necessary implication from the conferred powers, or (3) is clearly intended by the parties, as evidenced by the surrounding facts and circumstances.
- i. **Rest2d §1, 34**: A power of attorney is a written instrument by which one party, as principal, appoints another as agent and confers upon the latter the authority to perform certain specified acts or kinds of acts on behalf of the principal. A power of attorney instrument creates a principal-agent relationship.
- j. **Rest2d §34, comment h**: Because powers of attorney are ordinarily very carefully drafted and scrutinized, courts give the terms used a technical rather than a popular meaning. In additions, ambiguities in an instrument are resolved against the party who made it or caused it to be made, because that party had the better opportunity to understand and explain his meaning.
- k. **Rest2d §47**: the agent would be authorized to take such acts as the agent reasonably believes necessary to prevent substantial loss to the principal with respect to the interests committed to the agent's care.

C. Implied Actual Authority: authority implied from the words or conduct between the principal and the agent.
- a. Implied authority to act may arise from: (1) principal's words—incidental to express authority, (2) principal's conduct, (3) custom or usage, (4) emergency situation

b. Factors to determine whether a person hired under implied authority of an agent could be an employee
    i. Whether the agent reasonably believes because of present or past conduct of the principal that the principal wishes him to act in a certain way or to have certain authority.
    ii. The nature of the task or job
    iii. Implied authority may be necessary in order to implement the express authority.
    iv. The existence of prior similar practices
    v. Specific conduct by the principal in the past permitting the agent to exercise similar powers
c. The person alleging agency and resulting authority has the burden of proving that it exists
d. **Rest2d §78**: as a general rule, an agent is generally authorized to delegate the performance of incidental mechanical and ministerial acts, but may not delegate acts which involve discretion or the agent's special skill
e. **Rest2d §81**: As opposed to agents, servants generally have no implied authority to delegate their responsibilities
f. <u>Subagent</u>: a person that is appointed by an agent to perform functions undertaken by the agent for the principal. When the agent has authority to make such an appointment, the appointee is a subagent. The agent is primarily liable for the subagent, and the principal is secondarily liable.
    i. Note: If the agent is not authorized to appoint a subagent but nevertheless appoints a person to perform a function for the principal, the appointee is not a subagent, but rather the agent's agent, and the principal is not liable for the appointee
g. **Rest2d §5**: A subagent or servant is not only the agent or servant of the principal, but also the agent or servant of the appointing agent or servant.

D. Duty of Loyalty
    a. **Rest2d §390, comment c**: The agent must not take advantage of his position to persuade the principal into making a hard or improvident bargain. If the agent is one upon whom the principal naturally would rely for advice, the fact that the agent discloses that he is acting as an adverse party does not relieve him from the duty of giving the principal impartial advice based upon a carefully formed judgment as to the

principal interests. If he cannot or does not wish to do so, he has a duty to see that the principal secures the advice of a competent and disinterested third person. An agent who is in a close confidential relation to the principal, such as a family attorney, has a burden of proving that a substantial gift to him was not the result of undue influence.

b. **Rest2d §390**: Acting as an Adverse Party with Principal's Consent: an agent who, to the knowledge of the principal, acts on the agent's own account in a transaction in which the agent is employed has a duty to deal fairly with the principal and to disclose to him all facts with the agent knows or should know would reasonably affect the principal's judgment, unless the principal has manifested to the agent that the principal knows such facts or that the principal does not care to know them.

c. **Rest2d §390, comment a**: Before dealing with the principal on his own account, an agent has a duty to disclose to the principal all relevant facts fully and completely. A fact is relevant if it is one which the agent should realize would be likely to affect the judgment of the principal in giving his consent to the agent to enter into the particular transaction on the specified terms. So the disclosure must include not only the fact that the agent is acting on his own behalf, but also all other facts which he should realize have or are likely to have a bearing upon the desirability of the transaction form the viewpoint of the principal. This includes matters which a disinterested and skillful agent advising the principal would think reasonably relevant. The agent's duty of fair dealing is satisfied only if he reasonably believes that the principal understands the implications of the transaction.

d. *Schock v. Nash*, 1999: **VERY IMPORTANT CASE!!**
   i. <u>Bright Line Test</u>: where a power of attorney does not expressly authorize the attorney-in-fact to make gifts to himself, extrinsic evidence of the principal's intent to allow such gifts is not admissible. An attorney-in-fact may not make a gift to himself unless there is clear intent in writing from the principal allowing the gift. Oral authorization is not acceptable.
      1. Unless there is some specific unambiguous authorization to make a transaction that is in the fiduciaries self-interest it is voidable.

Agency & Partnership
SPARK LAW SERIES

2. Adopted in Texas.
ii. <u>Traditional Test</u>: a fiduciary's transfer to himself of trust property is voidable by the beneficiary unless (1) the transfer is approved by the court, (2) consented to by the settlor in advance, or (3) consent to by the beneficiary affected after full disclosure.
iii. Waiver of the fiduciary duty, to the extent that the P gives a blanket/general consent to A's crap. Waiver implies knowledge of all material facts and of one's rights, together with a willingness to refrain from enforcing those rights.
iv. The traditional equitable remedy against the agent is the constructive trust.
v. Trustee of grantor's estate and beneficiary under grantor's will brought action challenging transfers made by attorney-in-fact pursuant to durable power of attorney (POA). The Court of Chancery, New Castle County, ruled that attorney violated her fiduciary duty by transferring grantor's property to herself and her family, and ordered attorney and her family to pay restitution. Attorney appealed. The Supreme Court, Hartnett, J., held that:
   1. Attorney had burden to establish that grantor, after full disclosure of facts, consented to attorney's gratuitous transfers to herself and her family members;
   2. POA agreement did not give attorney express authority to transfer property to herself and her family, as required for such transfers to be valid;
   3. Even if POA had been ambiguous, extrinsic evidence did not support finding that attorney had authority to transfer grantor's assets to herself and her family; and
   4. Restitution orders issued against attorney's family members were supported by evidence, even if family members were unaware that transfers were improper.
   5. Constructive Trust – When appropriated funds have been used to purchase property

the court can require that this property be treated as being held in trust for the benefit of those form who it was appropriated.
6. The court may require an accounting of all receipts and disbursements by the fiduciary.
vi. Durable POA – survives the incapacity of the Principal
vii. The Grantor may consent to a fiduciary's gift (Active)
viii. The Grantor may waive his/her rights if the have all the pertinent knowledge of the facts and their rights and do nothing to void or halt the transaction
ix. Courts frown upon blanket consents. They will generally rule that each transaction requires its own authorization. In this case given that the POA was a boilerplate document from the bank the Ct found it was not a blanket authorization.

e. **Rogers v. Robson, Masters, Ryan, Brumund & Belom**
i. Rogers, doctor, named defendant in medical mal case; discovery shows that he was not negligent. He said that he did not want the case settled. The law firm settled the case anyway and the insurance company that was defending Roger is the same insurance company that was paying the law firm. Law firm continued to represent both the Dr. and the insurance company.
ii. Did the law firm have a duty to disclose the fact that they were going to settle? Yes, Why? Because there was two clients (Dr and insurance co. The right to be entitled to full disclosure stems from the atty-client relationship and this is not affected by the extent of insurer's authority to settle without the P's consent.
iii. No disclosure was made to the P and the P was not given the opportunity to elect what course to pursue, the court does not need to speculate what recourse, if any, plaintiff has under the terms of the insurance policy.
iv. What did he lose by having a settlement against him? His reputation, no insurance.
v. ABA rendered an ethics opinion on this issue: whether an lawyer hired by insured represents insured or both insurance co and insured; lawyer

loyalty to client and may represent both but if the insured does not want to settle, the atty must disclose the clients right to settle before settling for the ins. co.

    vi. Atty cannot get a blanket waiver at the beginning of the representation to be able to represent both. The Dr. cannot realistically understand what rights he might be waiving. This cannot be meaningful consent.

f. During the term of the agency, an agent may not, without the informed consent of the principal, act on behalf of persons whose interests conflict with those of the principal. The agent may not act on behalf of an adverse party in a transaction connected with the agency. In addition, the agent is prohibited from acting on behalf of any third person whose interests conflict with those of the principal, even if the third person is not engaging in a transaction with the principal. Of course, the corollary is that one may serve as a dual agent, provided that both principals are advised of the planned dual representation and have agreed to allow it. Bottom line: the agent must disclose when there is a conflict and must get consent.

SOURCES OF AGENCY POWER

Type of Power	How Created	Effect
Actual Authority • Express • Implied	Expressly granted by P to A Implied by P's words or conduct	A has the power and right to act for P (P is bound)
Apparent Authority	Holding out by P and reliance by third party	A has the power to act (P is bound) but not the right (A may be liable to P)
Estoppel	P's intentional or negligent causing of detrimental reliance by Third Party	A has no power to act (P is not bound) but P must compensate third party for losses

Agency & Partnership
SPARK LAW SERIES

Power of Agents to Bind the Firm by Unauthorized Acts

A. Introduction
   a. An agent's power to bind the principal is the agent's ability to do so. Authority is the power to bind that results from the principal's manifestations to the agent of the principal's consent to be bound.
   b. **Rest2d §8, §27, §34, §49**: An agent's power to bind the principal by an unauthorized action is based on the principal's manifestations—written or spoken words or other conduct—to third persons. However, a third person dealing with an agent has a correlative duty to act reasonably in interpreting the principal's conduct; the third person must reasonably believe, based on the principal's conduct and in light of all accompanying circumstances, that the principal consents to being bound by the particular act in question.
   c. Apparent authority CANNOT be based solely on the agent's conduct.
B. **An agent has the power to bind by unauthorized acts if**
   a. **Apparent Authority**
   b. **Estoppel to deny the agent was authorized**
   c. **Inherent Agency Power**
   d. **** On exam, run through each category and see if they apply****
C. Apparent Authority
   a. **Apparent authority all depends on what the third party believes**
      i. **(1) The P "holds out" that the agent has the authority – P's manifestation of consent,**
         1. "Holds out" can occur in 3 ways
            a. (1) By direct P to 3rd party communications (not in this case)
            b. (2) Appointment to a position with customary duties
            c. (3) Prior acts (practice or course of dealing) as between the parties.
      ii. **(2) 3rd party reasonably believed/relied that the P consents to A's authorization, AND**
      iii. **(3) The 3rd party must actually believe the agent is authorized.**

Agency & Partnership
SPARK LAW SERIES

    b. The burden of proof is on the person who wants the agency power to exist
    c. Apparent authority cannot be created by the agent's conduct.
    d. **Majority Rule** - The modern trend is to give the president of a corporate office both implied and apparent authority to conduct ordinary business transactions. Under both modern and traditional—By virtue of his position as Pres he has the authority to do anything in the ordinary course of business.
    e. **Minority Rule** – (including Tx) – There is no apparent authority by virtue of a Corporate position. If the Pres. runs the day to day operations of the business he has apparent authority to the powers normally associated with a Gen Mgr.
    f. **Rest2d §8b(1):** A person who is not otherwise liable as a party to a transaction purported to be done on his account, is nevertheless subject to liability to persons who have changed their positions because of their belief that the transaction was entered into by or for him if
        i. He intentionally or carelessly cause such belief, or
        ii. Knowing of such belief and that others might change their positions because of it, he did not take reasonable steps to notify them of the facts.
    g. Estoppel vs. Apparent Authority
        i. Estoppel can be based on omissions, not just affirmative conduct
        ii. While merely entering into a contract based on a reasonable belief of authority is sufficient to invoke apparent authority, it is not a change in position sufficient to invoke estoppel. So, in estoppel, while the conduct necessary to charge a principal is lower than in apparent authority, the third party must show something additional: a detrimental change in position.
D. Estoppel (Binding partners)
    a. **Elements:**
        i. **P intentionally or negligently acts to cause such belief (an affirmative act or omission)**
        ii. **Misleading appearance of authority**
        iii. **Third party must:**
            1. **Reasonably believe that the agent was authorized**
            2. **Change their position to their detriment**

Agency & Partnership
SPARK LAW SERIES

- a. Note: merely entering into a K is not enough to have changed position to detriment
- b. <u>Ostensible Authority Doctrine</u>: generic term states use to describe power to bind by an unauthorized act
- c. Mere possession does not give authority (UCC §2-403: merchants not required to show title)

E. Inherent Agency Power
- a. <u>Inherent agency power</u>: a term used to indicate the power of an agent which is derived not from authority, apparent authority, or estoppel, but solely from the agency relation and exists for the protection of persons harmed by or dealing with a servant or agent.
- b. There is no difference between inherent agency power of a general agent (that carries authority that is customary) and inherent authority
- c. <u>General agent</u>: an agent authorized to conduct a series of transactions *involving* a continuity of service
- d. <u>Special agent</u>: an agent that is not a general agent; an agent authorized to conduct a single transaction or a series of transactions *not involving* continuity of service.
- e. **Rest2d §194**: A general agent for an undisclosed principal authorized to conduct transactions subject to his principal to liability for acts done on his account, if usual or necessary in such transactions, although forbidden by the principal to do them.
- f. **Rest2d §161 Unauthorized Act of General Agent:** A general agent for a disclosed or partially disclosed principal subjects his principal to liability for acts done on his account which usually accompany or are incidental to transactions which the agent is authorized to conduct if, although they are forbidden by the principal, the other party reasonably believes that the agent is authorized to them and has no notice that is not so authorized.

F. Special Topics
- a. Agent Diversion of Funds
    - i. Assume we have a P and an A whose apparent authority authorizes him to collect from third party amounts due to P.
        1. Hypo 1: Assume there is an actually amount due to principal. Agent takes the money

and runs. P wants the $. Third party says he already paid. To what extent is the P responsible for monies paid the A?
2. Hypo 2: Agent misrepresents the amount due to P, and skims the excess. Third party finally realizes they overpaid, and they want P to pay back the overpayments. To what extent is the P responsible for monies paid the A?
3. **How do we proceed with these problems?** Keep these analyses separate.
    a. *Tort*: Was A acting within scope of employment? If yes, the P is responsible.
        i. Is master respondeat superior for servant's actions? Respondeat superior: Master liable without fault for torts of servant within scope of employment?
        ii. Factors to consider
            1. Why was he hired? Was he acting within his regular duties?
            2. Was A acting on his own behalf? Or was the act motivated, at least in part, to serve the master?
    b. *Contract*: Was A acting under apparent authority? If yes, the P could be responsible.
ii. **Rest2d §219**: (1) a master is vicariously liable for the torts of his servant that are committed within the scope of employment. (2) The master is not subject to liability for the torts of his servants acting outside the scope of employment unless... (d) The servant

Agency & Partnership
SPARK LAW SERIES

            purported to act or to speak on behalf of the principal and there was reliance upon apparent authority, or he was aided in accomplishing the tort by the existence of the agency relation.
       iii. **Rest2d §228**: in order to be within the scope of employment, the servant's conduct must be actuated, at least in part, by a purpose to serve the master.
       iv. Under Rest2d rules, a master is liable for the torts of his servant if the servant commits the tort while acting within the scope of his employment as defined by §228 or if §219(2) applies
       v. **Rest2d §261**: A principal who puts a servant or other agent in a position which enables the agent, while apparently acting within his authority, to commit a fraud upon third persons is subject to liability to such third persons for the fraud. Comment: The principal is subject to liability under the rule stated in this section although he is entirely innocent, has received no benefit from the transaction, and although the agent acted solely for his own purposes.
       vi. The proper inquiry for determining vicarious liability of a principal whose agent defrauds the principal's customer is the relationship between the principal and the customer.

Management and Conduct of Firm Business

A. Intro
  a. Party autonomy: gives parties the freedom to change or adapt the entity's native governance structure
  b. Suppletory or enabling: an entity's governance structure gives the parties wide discretion
  c. Regulatory or Mandatory: an entity's governance structure constrains party discretion; the structure regulates party autonomy by preventing them from choosing a different governance structure
B. Partnerships
  a. Partners as Agents
    i. Apparent Authority

Agency & Partnership
SPARK LAW SERIES

1. UPA
   a. **UPA §9(1) Partner Agent of Partnership as to Partnership Business:** (1) Every partner is an agent of the partnership for the purpose of its business, and the act of every partner, including the execution in the partnership name of any instrument, for apparently carrying on in the usual way the business of the partnership of which he is a member binds the partnership, unless the partner so acting has in fact no authority to act for the partnership in the particular matter, and the person with whom he is dealing has knowledge of the fact that he has no such authority.
2. RUPA
   a. **RUPA §103 Effect of Partnership Agreement; Nonwaivable Provisions.** Except for the stuff they can't contract out of, relations among the partners and between the partners and the partnership are governed by the partnership agreement. To the extent the partnership agreement does not otherwise provide, this [Act] governs relations among the partners and between the partners and the partnership.
      i. Delaware's Equivalent: §15-103
   b. **RUPA §301 Partner Agent of Partnership.** (1) Each partner is an agent of the partnership for the purpose of its business. An act of a partner, including the execution of an instrument in the partnership

name, for apparently carrying on in the ordinary course the partnership business or business of the kind carried on by the partnership binds the partnership, unless the partner had no authority to act for the partnership in the particular matter and the person with whom the partner was dealing knew or had received a notification that the partner lacked authority. (2) An act of a partner which is not apparently for carrying on in the ordinary course the partnership business or business of the kind carried on by the partnership binds the partnership only if the act was authorized by the other partners.
3. At common law, you have to distinguish between trading and non-trading. You have to decide what your business is.
    a. Trading (retail establishment; business of buying and selling products)
        i. Generally if you buy, you've got a wholesaler that you buy from; then you sell to customers
        ii. But you have to borrow money, so that you can have the money to buy the goods to sell
        iii. Ask: Is regularly borrowing money within the course of business? Is the agent authorized to do so?
    b. Non-Trading (companies that do not buy and sell)

Agency & Partnership
SPARK LAW SERIES

      4. One who asserts that the particular act of an agent is within the scope of the agent's authority has the burden of proving the extent of such authority.
      5. If A seeks to impose liability on B for the act of C on the theory that B held C out as having power to do such act, clearly the burden of establishing the facts which constitute such holding out is on A.
      6. "Holding out" is established by showing that the principal placed the agent in a position that ordinarily carries with it generally recognized powers. The agent will then have, as far as third parties are concerned, the power to do the things ordinarily done by one occupying such a position, unless the third party has knowledge of limitations on the powers of the agents.

   ii. Estoppel to deny Partnership
      1. **Elements of Estoppel to deny partnership**
         a. **Misleading conduct by person (to be estopped) that he is a partner**
         b. **Conduct by person that holds out or consents to representation to Π**
         c. **Third party must:**
            i. **Reasonably believe that the agent was authorized**
            ii. **Change their position to their detriment**
               Note: merely entering into a K is not enough to have changed position to detriment
      2. If the representation is privately made, it may be taken advantage of only by persons to whom it was made; if it was publicly made, anyone can make use of it.
      3. The statutory test for partnership by estoppel requires that (1) credit must have been extended on the basis of partnership

representations or (2) that the alleged partner must have made or consented to representations being made in a public manner whether or not such representations were actually communicated to the persons extending credit.
4. UPA
    a. **UPA §16 Partner by Estoppel.**
        i. (1) When a person, by words spoken or written or by conduct, represents himself, or consents to another representing him to any one, as a partner in an existing partnership or with one or more persons not actual partners, he is liable to any such person to whom such representation has been made, who has, on the faith of such representation, given credit to the actual or apparent partnership, and if he has made such representation or consented to its being made in a public manner he is liable to such person, whether the representation has or has not been made or communicated to such person so giving credit by or with the knowledge of the apparent partner making the representation or consenting to its being made. (a) When a partnership liability results, he is liable as though he were an actual member of the partnership. (b) When no partnership liability results, he is liable jointly with the other

ii. (2) When a person has been thus represented to be a partner in an existing partnership, or with one or more persons not actual partners, he is an agent of the persons consenting to such representation to bind them to the same extent and in the same manner as though he were a partner in fact, with respect to persons who rely upon the representation. Where all the members of the existing partnership consent to the representation, a partnership act or obligation results; but in all other cases it is the joint act or obligation of the person acting and the persons consenting to the representation.

5. RUPA
   a. **RUPA §308 Liability of Purported Partner.**
      i. If a person, by words or conduct, purports to be a partner, or consents to being represented by another as a partner, in a partnership or with one or more persons not partners, the purported partner is liable to a person to whom the representation is made, if that person, relying on the representation, enters into a transaction with the

actual or purported partnership. If the representation, either by the purported partner or by a person with the purported partner's consent, is made in a public manner, the purported partner is liable to a person who relies upon the purported partnership even if the purported partner is not aware of being held out as a partner to the claimant. If partnership liability results, the purported partner is liable with respect to that liability as if the purported partner were a partner. If no partnership liability results, the purported partner is liable with respect to that liability jointly and severally with any other person consenting to the representation.

ii. If a person is thus represented to be a partner in an existing partnership, or with one or more persons not partners, the purported partner is an agent of persons consenting to the representation to bind them to the same extent and in the same manner as if the purported partner were a partner, with respect to persons who enter into transactions in reliance upon the representation. If all of the partners of the existing partnership consent to the representation, a partnership

act or obligation results. If fewer than all of the partners of the existing partnership consent to the representation, the person acting and the partners consenting to the representation are jointly and severally liable.
iii. A person is not liable as a partner merely because the person is named by another in a statement of partnership authority.
iv. A person does not continue to be liable as a partner merely because of a failure to file a statement of dissociation or to amend a statement of partnership authority to indicate the partner's dissociation from the partnership.
v. Except as otherwise provided in subsections (a) and (b), persons who are not partners as to each other are not liable as partners to other persons.

b. Partners as Managers
   i. UPA
      1. **UPA §9 (2)-(4) Partner Agent of Partnership as to Partnership Business:**
         a. (2) An act of a partner which is not apparently for the carrying on of the business of the partnership in the usual way does not bind the partnership unless authorized by the other partners.
         b. (3) Unless authorized by the other partners or unless they have abandoned the business, one or

Agency & Partnership
SPARK LAW SERIES

more but less than all the partners have no authority to:
- i. Assign the partnership property in trust for creditors or on the assignee's promise to pay the debts of the partnership,
- ii. Dispose of the good-will of the business,
- iii. Do any other act which would make it impossible to carry on the ordinary business of a partnership,
- iv. Confess a judgment,
- v. Submit a partnership claim or liability to arbitration or reference.

c. (4) No act of a partner in contravention of a restriction on authority shall bind the partnership to persons having knowledge of the restriction.

2. **UPA §18(h) Rules Determining Rights and Duties of Partners**: Any difference arising as to ordinary matters connected with the partnership business may be decided by a majority of the partners; but no act in contravention of any agreement between the partners may be done rightfully without the consent of all the partners.

ii. If there's already an ordinary business practice, you need a new vote to change it.

iii. ***Covalt v. High***
1. Be careful with this case: the idea that the duty of loyalty is overcome by the equal rights of partners is <u>wrong</u>!
2. The status resulting from the formation of a partnership creates a fiduciary relationship between partners. The status of partnership requires of each member an

obligation of good faith and fairness in their dealings with one another, and a duty to act in furtherance of the common benefit of all partners in transactions conducted within the ambit of partnership affairs

3. If the partners are equally divided, those who forbid a change must have their way. One partner cannot either engage a new or dismiss an old servant against the will of his copartner; nor, if the lease of the partnership place of business expires, insist on renewing the lease and continuing the business at the old place.

4. The rule is different as to transactions between partners and third parties: In dealing with a third party, a partner has the authority to act on behalf of the partnership in the usual way, even without the consent of the other partner

5. If the partners are unable to agree and if the partnership agreement does not provide an acceptable means for settlement of this disagreement, the only course of action is to dissolve the partnership

6. Be sure to tell the person that they are no longer a partner

Agency & Partnership
SPARK LAW SERIES

EXAMPLES OF ORDINARY VS. EXTRAORDINARY BUSINESS

Ordinary Business Requiring Majority Vote	Extraordinary Business Requiring Unanimous Vote
<ul><li>Hiring an attorney to represent the partnership in litigation</li><li>Paying partnership bills</li><li>Borrowing money to run the partnership</li><li>Selling the partnership's inventory in the ordinary course of business</li><li>Doing any act necessary to carry on in the ordinary course the business of the partnership (hiring employees, leasing office space</li></ul>	<ul><li>Submitting the partnership to arbitration</li><li>Assigning partnership assets for the benefit of creditors</li><li>Confessing judgment against the partnership</li><li>Disposing of the partnership's goodwill</li><li>Doing any act that would make it impossible to carry on partnership business (like surrendering a necessary business license)</li></ul>

C. Corporations
  a. Shareholders have no right to participate in the management and conduct of partnership business
  b. Management of the business and affairs of a corporation is vested in its board of directors.
  c. The board of directors generally delegates the authority to run business of the corporation on a day-to-day basis to officers elected by the board of directors.
  d. Shareholders are not agents of the corporation.
  e. Shareholders (even as the whole group) have no right to instruct the board of directors or to interfere in its management of the corporation's business and affairs.
  f. The shareholders can affect corporate management in two respects
     i. They elect the persons who will constitute the board of directors
     ii. The board of directors cannot take certain extraordinary actions (like amending the articles of incorporation, merging the corporation, selling all or substantially all of the corporation's assets) without first getting shareholder approval.

Agency & Partnership
SPARK LAW SERIES

- g. Whenever shareholder or board of director action is required, that action can only be taken by a majority vote at a meeting
- h. Courts have been allowing all the shareholders of a small corporation some ability to interfere in the discretion of the board of directors, such as specifying the identity of officers or terms of their employment with the corporation.
- i. Small corporations are called "close corporations"
- j. Close corporation supplements: create a special statutory structure that authorized all the shareholders to enter into unanimous shareholder agreements with regard to the business and affairs of the corporation, and to do so without regard to the traditional role of the board of directors
- k. Unless shares of a corporation are publicly traded, its shareholders may, by unanimous shareholder agreement, elect out of the board-dominant governance structure and substitute their own governance structure.
    - i. Texas has adopted this rule.

D. Limited Partnerships
- a. General partners in LP's have the same rights and same obligations as partners in regular partnerships.
- b. Limited partners in LP's have no rights, by virtue of being limited partners, to participate in management or conduct of the partnership business.
- c. Voting Rights of Limited Partners
    - i. RULPA
        1. **RULPA §302 Voting**: Subject to §303, the partnership agreement may grant to all or a specified group of the limited partners the right to vote upon any matter.
- d. Limitations on Contractual Expansions of Limited Partners' Rights
    - i. Courts have held, without satisfactorily describing the standards by which to judge a limited partner's activities, that the following did not constitute taking part in the control of the business:
        1. Acting as foreman in the employ of the partnership, with the power to purchase parts as necessary without consulting the general partner, but without the power to extend credit without prior approval from

the general partner or deal with the partnership account,
2. Acting as a member of the board of directors of the partnership
3. Acting as sales manager in a new car sales department of the partnership without power to hire or fire, and, with power to order cars only with the general partner's approval, and, participating in the choice of key employees and giving a certain degree of advice

ii. Before the adoption of the ULPA, a limited partner could not be held liable for partnership obligations if the limited partner participated in the conduct of partnership business. ULPA §7 was intended to liberalize the law: a limited partner would not become liable as a general partner unless the limited partner participated in the control of the business (as opposed to merely participating generally).

iii. **Frigidaire Sales v. Union Properties**
1. Limited partners are not liable as general partners simply because they are active officers or directors, or are stockholders of a corporate general partner in a limited partnership.
2. Principles as to whether the corporate entity should be regarded or disregarded:
    a. If there is an overt intention to regard or disregard the corporate entity, effect will be given thereto unless so to do will violate a duty owing
    b. The overt intention is that of the corporation whose entity is sought to be disregarded or of the person or persons owning its stock and sought to be visited with the consequence of regard or disregard of the corporate entity.
    c. The duty owing must be owing to the person seeking to invoke the

doctrine, and such duty may arise from common law and equity, contract or statute.
3. No public policy requires a person who contributes to the capital of business, acquires an interest in the profits, and some degree of control over the conduct of the business, to become bound for the obligations of the business; provided creditors have no reason to believe at the time their credits were extended that such person was so bound.

iv. **RULPA §303(b) Liability to Third Partners... Limited Partner participating in the control of business**: A limited partner does not participate in the control of the business solely by doing one or more of the following:
1. Being a contractor, agent, or employee of the LP or of a GP, or by being an officer, director, or shareholder of a GP that is a corporation
2. Consulting and advising with respect to the business
3. Acting as surety for the LP
4. Pursing a derivative action in the right of the LP
5. Requesting or attending a meeting of partners
6. Voting on: dissolution, sale, debt, change in nature of the business, admission or removal of an LP or a GP, a transaction involving a conflict of interest, an amendment to the partnership, other matters related to the business.

E. Limited Liability Companies
a. **ULLCA §301(a) Agency of members and managers in member-management LLC**: (1) Each member is an agent of the LLC for the purpose of its business, and an act of a member, including the signing of an instrument in the company's name, for apparently carrying on in the ordinary course the company's business or business of the kind carried

on by the company binds the company, unless the member had no authority to act for the company in the particular matter and the person with whom the member was dealing knew or had notice that the member lacked authority. (2) An act of a member which is not apparently for carrying on in the ordinary course the company's business or business of the kind carried on by the company binds the company only if the act was authorized by the other members.
> i. The LLC business form was developed for the purpose of partnerships

b. **ULLCA §301(b) Agency of members and managers in manager-management LLC:** Subject to subsection (c), in a manager-managed company: (1) A member is not an agent of the company for the purpose of its business solely by reason of being a member. Each manager is an agent of the company for the purpose of its business, and an act of a manager, including the signing of an instrument in the company's name, for apparently carrying on in the ordinary course the company's business or business of the kind carried on by the company binds the company, unless the manager had no authority to act for the company in the particular matter and the person with whom the manager was dealing knew or had notice that the manager lacked authority. (2) An act of a manager which is not apparently for carrying on in the ordinary course the company's business or business of the kind carried on by the company binds the company only if the act was authorized under Section 404.

c. **ULLCA §404(c) Management of limited liability company:** The only matters of a member or manager-managed company's business requiring the consent of all of the members are: (1) the amendment of the operating agreement under Section 103; (2) the authorization or ratification of acts or transactions under Section 103(b)(2)(ii) which would otherwise violate the duty of loyalty; (3) an amendment to the articles of organization under Section 204; (4) the compromise of an obligation to make a contribution under Section 402(b); (5) the compromise, as among members, of an obligation of a member to make a contribution or return money or other property paid or distributed in violation of this [Act]; (6) the making of interim distributions under Section 405(a), including the redemption

Agency & Partnership
SPARK LAW SERIES

of an interest; (7) the admission of a new member; (8) the use of the company's property to redeem an interest subject to a charging order; (9) the consent to dissolve the company under Section 801(b)(2); (10) a waiver of the right to have the company's business wound up and the company terminated under Section 802(b); (11) the consent of members to merge with another entity under Section 904(c)(1); and (12) the sale, lease, exchange, or other disposal of all, or substantially all, of the company's property with or without goodwill.
   d. Note: a recent case out of state, the statute said that something could be done by a vote of the members, and a member held enough votes did something by himself, and took the position that a majority of the members consented... the court said that Vote ≠ Consent and there should have been a meeting
   e. Delaware LLC §18-402 Management of limited liability company:
      i. Default: member management
      ii. Voting by profits, not by members (this is not uniform)

Managerial Discretion and Fiduciary Duties

A. Business Judgment Rule
   a. <u>Judgmental immunity</u>: an attorney who acts in good faith and in an honest belief that his advice and acts are well founded and in the best interest of his client is not answerable for a mere error of judgment or for a mistake in a point of law which has not been settled by the court of last resort in his state and on which reasonable doubt may be entertained by well-informed lawyers
      i. Judgmental Immunity requires good faith and honest belief. The good faith is subjective. Under judgmental immunity, you're not liable for a mere error of judgment.
         1. Standard of care: what a reasonably prudent attorney from your locale would do.
      ii. If a client is to meaningfully make a decision, he needs to have the information necessary to assess

the risks and benefits of either settling or proceeding to trial.
    iii. A lawyer should exert his best efforts to ensure that decisions of a client are made only after the client has been informed of relevant considerations.
    iv. Where there are reasonable alternatives, the lawyer should inform the client that the issue is uncertain, unsettled, or debatable, and allow the client to make the decision.
    v. The doctrine of Judgmental Immunity does not apply to an attorney's failure to inform a client of unsettled legal issues relevant to a settlement. Whether an attorney is negligent for such a failure is determined by whether the attorney exercised the same skill, knowledge, and diligence as attorneys of ordinary skill and capacity commonly possess and exercise in the performance of all other legal tasks. At the same time, an attorney's ultimate recommendation in an area of unsettled law is immune from suit.
b. Given an unsettled legal question and if reasonable lawyers could go the other way, then the lawyer won't be liable for a mistake in point of law.
c. Texas: no subjective good faith excuse in Texas. Your defense is what a reasonably prudent practitioner would do
    i. There is no subjective good faith excuse for attorney negligence. A lawyer in Texas is held to the standard of care which would be exercised by a reasonably prudent attorney.
    ii. Allowing the attorney to assert his subjective good faith, when the acts he pursues are unreasonable as measured by the reasonably competent practitioner standard, creates too great a burden for wronged clients to overcome.
    iii. If an attorney makes a decision which a reasonably prudent attorney could make in the same or similar circumstance, it is not an act of negligence even if the result is undesirable.
    iv. An attorney who makes a reasonable decision in the handling of a case may not be held liable if the decision later proves to be imperfect

d. **Rest2d §479(1) Paid Agent:** Unless otherwise agreed, a paid agent is subject to a duty to the principal to act with standard care and with the skill which is standard in the locality for the kind of work which the agent is employed to perform and, in addition, to exercise any special skill that the agent has.
e. What happens when the fiduciary's exercise of judgment leads to a loss?
    i. On one hand, no fiduciary has perfect foresight and perfect knowledge; even an ordinarily skillful, competent, and careful fiduciary will make decisions that will seem improper in the harsh glare of hindsight. No fiduciary should be made into a guarantor or insurer of a favorable result.
    ii. On the other hand, if a duty of care is to have any meaningful substantive content, a fiduciary should be held accountable for a failure to act with ordinary skill, competence, and care.
f. Directors are entitled to exercise their honest business judgment on the information before them, and to act within their corporate powers. That they may be mistaken, that other courses of action might have differing consequences, or that their action might benefit some shareholders more than others present no basis for the superimposition of judicial judgment, so long as it appears that the directors have been acting in good faith.
    i. Rationales:
        1. Director's room, rather than the courtroom, is the place to make decisions
        2. The court should not be making business decisions for a company
        3. The directors have enough things to deal with
g. In actions by stockholders, which assail the acts of their directors or trustees, courts will not interfere unless the powers have been illegally or unconscientiously executed, or unless it be made to appear that the acts were fraudulent or collusive and destructive of the rights of the stockholders. Mere errors of judgment are not sufficient as grounds for equity interference; for the powers of those entrusted with corporate management are largely discretionary.

h. The question of whether or not a dividend is to be declared or a distribution of some kind should be made is exclusively a matter of business judgment for the board of directors. Courts will not interfere with such discretion unless it is first made to appear that the directors have acted or are about to act in bad faith and for a dishonest purpose. It is for the directors to say, acting in good faith of course, when and to what extent dividends shall be declared.
i. Directors can be sued for the neglect of, or failure to perform, or other violation of his duties in the management and disposition of corporate assets committed to his charge. "Neglect" here is neglect of duties, not misjudgment.
j. The law of corporate fiduciary duties and remedies for violation of those duties are distinct from the aspirational goals of ideal corporate governance practices. Aspirational ideals of good corporate governance practices for boards of directors that go beyond the minimum legal requirements of the corporation law are highly desirable, often tend to benefit stockholders, sometimes reduce litigation and can usually help directors avoid liability. But they are not required by the corporation law and do not define standards of liability.
k. As applied in evaluating the decisions of corporate officers or directors, the business judgment rule protects them from liability on account of business judgments made in good faith:
    i. **Business Judgment Rule**: **a director or officer who makes a business judgment in good faith fulfills his duty of care if:**
        1. **He is not interested in the subject of his business judgment**
        2. **He is informed with respect to the subject of his business judgment to the extent he reasonably believes necessary, and**
        3. **He rationally believes that his business judgment is in the best interests of the corporation**
l. Delaware: requires (1) gross negligence and (2) an improper primary business purpose
m. Negligence in the management of the affairs of a general partnership or joint venture does not create any right of action against that partner by other members of the partnership. It is only when there is a breach of trust, such as

when one partner or joint venturer holds property or assets belonging to the partnership or venture, and converts such to his own use, would such action lie. In ordinary management and operation of a general partnership or joint venture there is no liability to the other partners or joint venturers for the negligence in the management or operation of the affairs of the enterprise.
n. Management of the business necessarily includes decisions regarding the management of profits, unless the parties have specified otherwise in the limited partnership agreement
o. A limited partner's position is analogous to that of a corporate shareholder, whose role is that of an investor with limited liability, and with no voice in the operation of the enterprise. A general partner's relationship to the limited partners is analogous to the relationship of a corporate board of directors to the corporate shareholders; the general partner functions as a fiduciary with a duty of good faith and fair dealing. Like the corporate director's fiduciary responsibility to the shareholders for the declaration of dividends, the general partner's duty to the limited partners in the distribution of profit is discharged by decisions made in good faith that reflect legitimate business concerns.
p. Shareholders of a public corporation who disagree with a board of directors' management have two remedies: they can elect different directors, or they can sell their shares
q. **RUPA §404 General Standards of Partner's Conduct:**
    i. (a) The only fiduciary duties a partner owes to the partnership and the other partners are the duty of loyalty and the duty of care set forth in subsections (b) and (c).
    ii. (b) A partner's duty of loyalty to the partnership and the other partners is limited to the following:
        1. To account to the partnership and hold as trustee for it any property, profit, or benefit derived by the partner in the conduct and winding up of the partnership business or derived from a use by the partner of partnership property, including the appropriation of a partnership opportunity;
        2. To refrain from dealing with the partnership in the conduct or winding up of the

Agency & Partnership
SPARK LAW SERIES

       partnership business as or on behalf of a party having an interest adverse to the partnership; and
      3. To refrain from competing with the partnership in the conduct of the partnership business before the dissolution of the partnership.
    iii. (c) A partner's duty of care to the partnership and the other partners in the conduct and winding up of the partnership business is limited to refraining from engaging in grossly negligent or reckless conduct, intentional misconduct, or a knowing violation of law.
    iv. This is a Gross negligence approach

B. Duty of Loyalty
  a. **Starr v. International Realty**
    i. Where one partner on purchases which he has made on behalf of the partnership withholds a secret discount, the entire amount of the discount must be accounted for.
    ii. The partner receiving secret commissions on the partnership transactions must account for the whole amount of the commissions so received even though he may have been assisted in the deal by a third person, to whom he paid a part of such commissions.
  b. **UPA §21(1) Partner Accountable as a Fiduciary**: Every partner must account to the partnership for any benefit, and hold as trustee for it any profits derived by him without the consent of the other partners from any transaction connected with the formation, conduct, or liquidation of the partnership or from any use by him of its property.
  c. TRPA art 6132b-4.04(a)(1), (b), (e), (f) General Standards of Partner's Conduct
  d. Is there a cause of action against the general partner for breach of fiduciary duty? Would allowing this lawsuit mean that general partners can't manage?
  e. What is the standard of review of the fiduciary duties?
    i. The business judgment rule (which gives the Π the burden to prove there was self dealing, or informed deliberate actions, which probably includes gross

negligence, or that there was bad faith)? Under the business judgment rule, Π's claim is valid.
1. Here there is no self-dealing, because distributions affect each partner equally; there are deliberate acts; is there bad faith?
ii. There are three things that are badges of bad faith:
1. A transaction without a legitimate business purpose
2. The transaction had an improper primary purpose
3. The transaction was waste or fraud
iii. Fairness is the standard of review for self-dealing transactions. One of the ways you show fairness is fairness in dealing and fairness in price.
f. In any fiduciary relationship, the burden of proof shifts to the fiduciary to show by clear and convincing evidence that a transaction is equitable and just.
g. Where there is a question of breach of a fiduciary duty of a managing partner, all doubts will be resolved against him, and the managing partner has the burden of proving his innocence
h. The general partner's duty to the limited partners in the distribution of profit is discharged by decisions made in good faith that reflect legitimate business concerns
i. **Rest2d §13, comment a:** The agreement on behalf of a principal causes the agent to be a fiduciary, that is, a person having a duty, created by his undertaking, to act primarily for the benefit of another in matters connected with his undertaking.
j. Problem 7.5
i. The LLC contract included a section which said you could participate in other companies, even competing ones
ii. Arguments
1. How should that contract provision be interpreted?
a. Ohio court said that the provision was not ambiguous and should be interpreted to allow members of the LLC to compete against the LLC
2. Was there a waiver of

3. Were their other fiduciary duties that would keep him from acting this way?
k. **ULLCA §101(10) Manager:** a person, whether or not a member of a manager-managed company, who is vested with authority under §301
l. **ULLCA §103(b)**
    i. The comment says that under (b)(2) and (b)(4), an irreducible core of fiduciary responsibilities survive any contrary provision in the operating agreement.
m. **ULLCA §409**
    i. Especially (b)(3)
    ii. §(b)(1) "Business Opportunity Doctrine": certain business opportunities are treated as belonging to the beneficiary. As the property of the beneficiary, the fiduciary's duty of loyalty prohibits the fiduciary from misappropriating such business opportunities. This doctrine lets the fiduciary to take the business opportunity when the beneficiary has declined to pursue it.
n. Delaware LLC §302 Classes and Voting (Members)
o. Delaware LLC §404 Classes and Voting (Managers)
p. Delaware LLC §1101
q. Converting the partnership to a real estate investment trust is subject to the fairness standard of review.
r. Unless limited by the partnership agreement, the general partner has the fiduciary duty to manage the partnership in its interest and in the interests of the limited partners. This shows a marriage of common law fiduciary duties to contract theory when it comes to considering actions undertaken in the limited partnership context
s. A claim of breach of fiduciary duty must be analyzed first in terms of the operative governing instrument—the partnership agreement—and only where that document is silent or ambiguous, or where principles of equity are implicated, will a Court begin to look for guidance from the statutory default rules, traditional notions of fiduciary duties, or other extrinsic evidence
t. The court does not apply the fiduciary duty here because the partnership agreement says that to merge, there must be limited partners' consent.
u. You must make full disclosure to get consent.

Agency & Partnership
SPARK LAW SERIES

- v. Fiduciary duties include full disclosure. One must act fairly to get consent... which means full disclosure.
- w. To what extent should fiduciaries be allowed to contract around fiduciary duties?
    - i. <u>Traditional Approach</u>: fiduciary duties are mandatory, and simply by being a partner, one owes the other partners and the partnership certain duties. Except for narrow and specific waivers following full disclosure, those status-based fiduciary duties are not amendable by the parties.
    - ii. <u>Hypothetical Bargain Approach</u>: business relationships and entities are contractual. Fiduciary duties can be characterized as a hypothetical bargain—that is, contract terms the parties themselves would have agreed to in the absence of transaction costs. Applying the hypothetical bargain approach to fiduciary duties suggests that these duties are waivable.
- x. So can you contract out of fiduciary duties?
    - i. *Sonet I*: fiduciary duties could be contracted out of in cases where the LP's were going to vote
        1. Trial court
    - ii. *Sonet II*: Cannot contract out of duty, because when seeking the LP's vote, there is a fiduciary duty to give full disclosure to the LP's
        1. Trial court
    - iii. *Gotham* (*Sonet* notes from website) court: you can restrict but not eliminate them; but this case only dealt with contractual fiduciary duties.
        1. But if you have to contract into these duties, why can't you contract out of them?
        2. Supreme Court
    - iv. ULLCA §103(b) says no.
- y. Fairness is part of the fiduciary duty
- z. Fairness Test (Δ has burden of proof)
    - i. Arms length Dealing? (look at how the agreement came about)
    - ii. Fair price? (FMV: how much a third party would pay at arm's length transaction with no coercion)
- aa. What remedies are available for breach of fiduciary duty? All common law remedies that would be available for breach of

fiduciary duties... unless the contract specifically limited the remedies available.

Firm's Accountability for Notification to and Knowledge of the Agent

A. General Rules
   a. Knowledge
      i. The knowledge of an employee may be imputed to an employer under an employee dishonesty insurance policy if the employee holds a position of management or control in the exercise of which a duty to report known dishonesty of a fellow employee can be found to exist either explicitly or by fair inference from a course of conduct.
      ii. **Rest2d §272:** A principal is affected by the knowledge of an agent either (i) when the knowledge concerns a matter within the scope of the agent's power to bind the principal or (ii) when the agent has a duty to give the principal that information.
      iii. **Rest2d §273:** A principal will not be affected by an agent's knowledge concerning a matter outside the scope of the agent's actual authority, but within the agent's apparent authority, unless a third person has relied on the agent's apparent authority.
      iv. **Rest2d §381, cmt a:** An agent has a duty to inform the principal of information learned by the agent that relates to the matters entrusted to the agent by the principal: an agent may have a duty to act upon, or to communicate to his principal information which the agent has received, although not specifically instructed to do so. The duty exists if the agent has notice of facts which, in view of the agent's relations with the principal, the agent should know may affect the desires of the agent's principal as to the agent's own conduct or the conduct of the principal or of another agent. This duty is inferred from the agent's position, just as authority is inferred. The extent of the duty depends upon the kind of work entrusted to the agent, the agent's previous relations with the principal, and all the facts of the situation.

v. **Rest2d §9, cmt c:** Knowledge of a fact is limited to actual conscious awareness of it.
vi. **Rest2d §9(1):** Persons have notice of a fact when they know it, have reason to know it, should know it, or have been notified of it.
vii. **Rest2d §9(3):** The rules regarding attributing to the principal an agent's knowledge also apply to the attribution of notice
viii. **Rest2d §268, cmt d:** If the state of mind of a principal in a transaction is a factor, a notification by a third person giving information to an agent who does not communicate it to the principal does not operate with like effect as a similar notification given to the principal.
ix. **Rest2d §275, cmt b:** In many situations, in order for one to be responsible, it is necessary that the act should be done with knowledge in a subjective sense, and it is not sufficient that one has means of information.
x. A principal will not necessarily be held responsible for an agent's knowledge for all purposes.
xi. Knowledge and Notice
    1. UPA §3
    2. RUPA §102(f)
    3. Re-RULPA §103
    4. ULLCA §102
b. Notification
    i. Timing
        1. Knowledge
            a. P is responsible only after reasonable time to communicate to the P and P has had reasonable time to act on the info... not when A learned
            b. If organizational P, reasonable time to communicate includes time to go from agent 1 to P and then from P to agent 2. Assuming agent 1 has knowledge and agent 2 is about to act. We consider also if the organization has reasonable procedures and reasonable diligence in following procedures.

2. Notification
    a. Legal act to bind.
    b. Does communication with A bind the principal? This assumes the A is authorized or apparently authorized.
    c. P is bound at the time the notification was communicated to the agent
    d. If some response from P is required, P is allowed reasonable time to act
    e. Ex: K says repaint after renewal of lease
        i. Renewal is effective when A got communication from tenant
        ii. P has time to set up painting services
  ii. A notification given to an agent is notice to the principal if it is given to an agent authorized to receive it or to an agent apparently authorized to receive it.
  iii. Knowledge and Notice vs. Notification
      1. Knowledge and Notice involve responsibility for *awareness* of information
      2. Notification is a formal act intended in itself to determine the rights of the parties, regardless of the degree of knowledge of the recipient
  iv. Question of the effectiveness of a notification to an agent: Did the notification bind the principal?
  v. **Rest2d §268**: Notification to an agent is notification to the principal if the agent was actually or apparently authorized to receive the notification.
  vi. **Rest2d §273**: Knowledge that is only within an agent's apparent authority will not be attributed to the principal unless a third party relied on the appearance of authority.
  vii. **Rest2d §283**: The question of the effect of notification, knowledge, and notice is not limited to

principals and agents. A master will be affected by notification to, or knowledge or notice of, a servant so long as the servant had a duty to act on or communicate the information or notification as a part of the servant's employment or apparent employment.
- B. Time from which Notification or Knowledge Affects Principal
  - a. **Rest2d §213 Principal Negligent or Reckless:** A person conducting an activity through servants or other agents is subject to liability for harm resulting from his conduct if he is negligent or reckless:
    - i. (a) In giving improper or ambiguous orders of in failing to make proper regulations; or
    - ii. (b) In the employment of improper persons or instrumentalities in work involving risk of harm to others:
    - iii. (c) In the supervision of the activity; or
    - iv. (d) In permitting, or failing to prevent, negligent or other tortious conduct by persons, whether or not his servants or agents, upon premises or with instrumentalities under his control.
  - b. **Rest2d §213, cmt d**: An employee must have some antecedent reason to believe that the employee presents an undue risk of harm to others because of his vicious nature
  - c. **Rest2d §278:** Before a principal may be charged with an agent's knowledge or notice, the agent must have had both a reasonable time to communicate the information to the principal, and the principal must have had a reasonable opportunity to act on it.
  - d. **UCC §1-207(27):** Notice, knowledge or a notice or notification received by an organization is effective for a particular transaction from the time when it is brought to the attention of the individual conducting that transaction, *and in any event from the time when it would have been brought to his attention if the organization had exercised due diligence*. An organization exercises due diligence if it maintains reasonable routines for communicating significant information to the person conducting the transaction and there is reasonable compliance with the routines. Due diligence does not require an individual acting for the organization to communicate information unless such communication is part of his regular

duties or unless he has reason to know of the transaction and that the transaction would be materially affected by the information.
- e. **Rest2d §270**: Because notification is a legal act intended to be effective in and of itself, notification to an authorized or apparently authorized agent is effective immediately. As to the informational aspects of a notification, notice is also effective immediately. However where the principal is required to act on account of the notification, the principal is allowed reasonable time for the agent to communicate the fact of notification, as well as reasonable time to act on the notification.

C. Adverse Agents
- a. General Rule: Principal's rights are not affected by knowledge of adverse agent
- b. Rationale: agent's interests conflict with principal's so agent won't tell principal what he needs to know
- c. There are several definitions of adverse agent
    - i. Agent tried to defraud principal and third party
    - ii. Rest2d §282's
    - iii. Agent's relations to the subject matter are so adverse as to practically destroy the relationship
- d. <u>Doctrine of Adverse Domination</u>: corporations only act through their officers and directors, and those officers and directors cannot be expected to sue themselves or to initiate any action contrary to their own interests
    - i. Rationale: it is impossible for the corporation to bring the action while it is controlled by culpable officers and directors
    - ii. Two versions of the Doctrine
        1. <u>Disinterested Majority</u>: If board of directors is sufficiently dominated by adverse directors, the corporation is not treated as having known
            - a. What is sufficiently dominated?
                - i. Majority view: a majority of directors are adverse
                - ii. Minority view: the entire board is adverse... if one innocent guy knows, the entire corporation knows

- b. A plaintiff benefits from a presumption that the cause of action does not accrue or the statute of limitations does not run so long as the culpable directors remain the majority
- c. Defendant can rebut that presumption with evidence that someone other than the wrongdoing directors had knowledge of the basis for the cause of action, combined with the ability and the motivation to bring an action.
2. <u>Single Disinterested Director</u>: if there is one director with knowledge in a board of directors and that director is adverse, P is not responsible
    - a. Statutes of limitations are tolled only so long as there is no director with knowledge of facts giving rise to possible liability who could have induced the corporation to bring an action.
    - b. Plaintiff has the burden of showing that the culpable directors had full, complete, and exclusive control of the corporation, and must negate the possibility that an informed director could have induced the corporation to sue.
iii. <u>Minority View</u>: Doctrine not recognized because it is inconsistent with applicable state law tolling doctrines and policies strictly construing statutes of limitations.
iv. <u>Adverse Interest Exception</u>: a corporation is charged with knowledge of what its agent knows, unless the agent's relations to the subject matter are so adverse as to practically destroy the relationship, as when the agent is acting in his own interest and adversely to that of his principal, or is secretly

engaged in attempting to accomplish a fraud which would be defeated by a disclosure to his principal.
1. The subject matter to be considered when evaluating the degree of the director's adverse interest is the decision whether to make a claim, not the underlying acts that gave rise to that claim.
v. **Rest2d §279:** The principal is not affected by the knowledge of an agent as to matters involved in a transaction in which the agent deals with the principal as an adverse party
vi. Knowledge of the wrongdoing directors or officers of facts that would give rise to legal liability to the corporation on the part of those directors or officers will not be imputed to the corporation so long as those directors or officers control the corporation.

e. As a general rule, shareholders must defer to the power of the board of directors to bring a derivative suit, by demanding that the board bring suit on the corporation's behalf. Derivative suits are permitted only where the board of directors is incapable of discharging its responsibility to manage the suit.

f. **Revised Model Business Corporation Act (RMBCA) §7.42:** Unless the corporation is threatened with irreparable harm, shareholders must demand that the board act and wait 90 days before bringing a derivative suit

g. **RMBCA §7.44:** Whether the shareholder may thereafter bring suit depends on whether an independent, disinterested, body (majority of the board, committee, or a court-appointed panel) decided, after a reasonable investigation, that a suit was not in the best interest of the corporation.

h. **Rest2d §271:** The adverse agent is another context in which the rules regarding notification differ from those regarding knowledge and notice. Notification by a third person given to an agent acting adversely to the principal is effective unless the third person has notice the agent is acting adversely.

i. Presumably the basis for the different in treatment is that, in the case of notification, the third person is reasonably relying on the authority or apparent authority of the agent to act for the principal in receiving the notification.

Agency & Partnership
SPARK LAW SERIES

NOTIFICATION VS. KNOWLEDGE

	Notification	Knowledge
Defined	An act calculated to give information to another that affects the legal relationship between the parties	Subjective awareness of a particular fact or condition
Authority Required for Imputation	Principal will be charged with notification given to agent if agent had any type of authority in the transaction to receive notification.	Principal will be charged with agent's knowledge only if agent had actual authority in the transaction to affect principal's rights.
Duration	Continues indefinitely—does not become ineffective because of the passage of time.	May become ineffective because of the passage of time.
Effect of Adverse Agent	Notification still imputed to principal unless third party knew agent was acting adversely.	Knowledge not imputed to principal because agent was acting outside the scope of actual authority.

Ratification of Unauthorized Transactions

A. The doctrine of ratification arises out of the risk of unintended dealings inherent in the use of agents in the marketplace. Even where an agent dealing with a third party has acted outside the scope of the agent's power to bind the principal, the principal may nevertheless be bound if the principal ratifies the agent's act.

B. Affirmance
    a. Marital status cannot in and of itself prove the agency relationship. The fact that one spouse tends more to business matters than the other does not, absent other evidence of agreement or authorization, constitute the delegation of power as to an agent.
    b. No implied or apparent authority to act on behalf of spouse just because married
    c. **Rest2d §82:**

Agency & Partnership
SPARK LAW SERIES

   i. Definition: Ratification is defined as the affirmance by a principal of a prior act which <u>did not bind</u> P but which was done ore professedly done on his account.
      1. Professedly done: the A said he was acting on behalf of P
   ii. Ratification requires acceptance of the results of the act with an intent to ratify, and with full knowledge of all the material circumstances.
   iii. The ratification relates back to the time of the actual act.
d. **Rest2d §98**: Before the receipt of benefits may constitute ratification, the other requisites for ratification must first be present. Thus if the original transaction was not purported to be done on account of the principal, the fact that the principal receives its proceeds does not make him a party to it.
e. **Rest2d §85 and 87**: A person (the ratifier) only has the right to ratify the act of another (the actor) where (i) the actor purported to act as an agent, and (ii) the actor either identified the ratifier as the principal or intended to act on account of the ratifier.
   i. Ratification is not available if there is an undisclosed P
f. **Rest2d §104**: Despite these limitations on the power to ratify an unauthorized transaction, nothing prevents the would-be ratifier from entering into a separate, new contract with the third party.
g. **How you affirm something: Rest2d §83**: a principal may affirm a transaction either by electing to be bound or by conduct. For an implied affirmance by conduct, the conduct must be such that it can only be justified if the principal is electing to affirm the transaction
h. Actual affirmance: "I affirm the contract"
i. Implied affirmance: conduct that shows affirmance... accepting benefits of the K. See Rest2d §98.
j. One type of conduct constituting an affirmance is the knowing acceptance by the principal of benefits of the transaction.
k. **Rest2d §98**: For acceptance of benefits to constitute affirmance, the principal must have no claim to the accepted

benefits other than through or under the transaction in question
l. **Rest2d §91 Knowledge of Principal at Time of Affirmance: (Avoiding affirmance)**
   i. (1) If, at the time of affirmance, the purported principal is ignorant of material facts involved in the original transaction, and is unaware of his ignorance, he can thereafter avoid the effect of the affirmance.
   ii. (2) Material facts are those which substantially affect the existence or extent of the obligations involved in the transaction, as distinguished from those which affect the values or inducements involved in the transaction.
   iii. §91 restated: If the ratifier does not have actual knowledge of material facts, but only reason to know them, then the ratifier may avoid the affirmance.
   iv. The law is clear that for ratification of an unauthorized act to occur so as to bind the principal he must have actual knowledge of the material facts being adopted at the time affirmance occurs. Absent such knowledge, an affirmance may be avoided upon the principal's learning the material facts.
   v. The general rules holding a principal accountable for the knowledge of an agent apply in a ratification context to prevent the ratifier from avoiding the affirmance.
   vi. Ex: A enters into unauthorized K with 3rd party; P affirms. But there was a material fact A didn't tell P. Is P responsible for what A knew? No. If there is a 2nd agent that knows, P may be responsible.
m. In order to ratify, a principal must have been able to undertake the transaction both at the earlier time when the agent acted and at the later time of the act of ratification. In addition, a principal cannot ratify a transaction which the principal does not have the authority to enter at the time of the attempted ratification.
   i. This is also important to the inquiry of whether ratification is possible

Agency & Partnership
SPARK LAW SERIES

- n. Ratification of prior unauthorized acts can form the basis for a claim of apparent authority.
    - i. Suppose an agent enters into an unauthorized transaction which the principal ratifies without indicating to the third party that the agent had acted without authority. Suppose further that the same third party again deals with the agent, and the agent again exceeds authority in a similar fashion. The principal may be bound to the second contract on the basis of the apparent authority created by the manifestation to the third party that the agent had authority to deal.
- o. **Rest2d §91, cmt e, illustration 15**: Purporting to represent P but without authority, A leases P's farm to T for five years, a not unusual term. A writes to P, informing him of all the terms except the duration of the lease. P replies: "Send me the rent." There is ratification of all the terms and P cannot avoid the obligations of the lease.

C. Knowledge of Agents
   a. As a general rule, the knowledge of an agent acting within the scope of his authority is chargeable to the principal, regardless of whether that knowledge is actually communicated
   b. **Rest2d §94, cmt a**: In certain circumstances it is possible for silence to be construed as an affirmance resulting in ratification.
   c. Affirmance alone will not necessarily bind a principal who acts upon incomplete or inaccurate information.
   d. **Rest2d §280**: The principal will not be charged with an agent's knowledge of facts relating to the agent's own unauthorized acts. **STRESSED FOR EXAM!!!**
   e. An agent acting in an unauthorized manner means the agent breached fiduciary duty
   f. Ratification by P waives fiduciary duty, i.e. the agent is exonerated of his breach
   g. HYPO: Agent acts without authority and enters into lease with third party for years. A tells P about lease, but not about the 5 years. Length of term is a material fact, so he could get out of it... but shouldn't P have inquired as to the length? P assumed the risk as to standard terms. (Rosin said)
   h. UPA §12... what are the TRPA and RUPA equivalents?

Agency & Partnership
SPARK LAW SERIES

Approach to Ratification

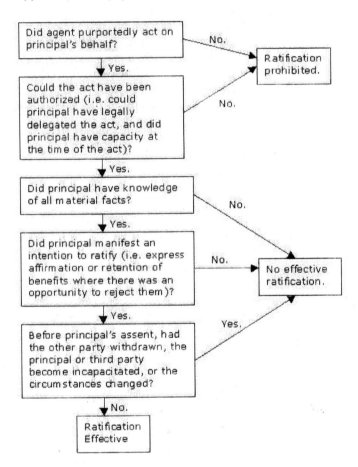

Ownership of the Firm

    A. For this chapter, focus on how UPA, RUPA, TRPA compare
    B. Ownership of the firm vs. Ownership of the Assets
        a. Can't transfer your rights to specific partnership property.
        b. Rights in all of the partnership property is called: interest in partnership

c. Construes this as an assignment of an interest in the partnership, but not an interest in the assets—so this assigns all your claims.
d. UPA, RUPA, and TRPA treat specific partnership property the same way
e. UPA and RUPA are equivalent for transfers of interests too
f. UPA says "interest in the partnership"; RUPA says "transferable interest in the partnership"
g. UPA
   i. UPA §8
   ii. UPA §17
   iii. UPA §24
   iv. UPA §25
      1. (1) says what your rights are
      2. (2)(c) says specific partnership property is not subject to attachment or execution, except on a claim against the partnership
      3. Tenancy in Partnership: this is not co-tenant, joint tenants, etc... so what is it? §25(2) lists the attributes of a T-in-P.
      4. (2)(a) right to possess for partnership purposes only
      5. (2)(b) right to specific partnership property is not separately assignable
      6. (2)(d): when a partner dies, this property goes to surviving partners
      7. (2)(e): no marital rights in specific partnership property
   v. UPA §26
   vi. UPA §27 says what happens when you assign your intrest
   vii. Profits and surplus are not defined
      1. Surplus: property that's not needed for partnership purposes
      2. When would you not need it? Dissolution
   viii. What is a beneficial interest? Define and put on page 7 of statute book!!!!!!
   ix. UPA §8 defines partnership property
   x. UPA §18 = RUPA §401
   xi. UPA §25(2) = RUPA §502
h. RUPA

Agency & Partnership
SPARK LAW SERIES

      i. RUPA §101(3)
     ii. RUPA §101(9)
    iii. RUPA §101(10)
    iv. RUPA §203
     v. RUPA §204
    vi. RUPA §501
   vii. RUPA §502

DETERMINING WHETHER PROPERTY IS PARTNERSHIP PROPERTY
Under the RUPA

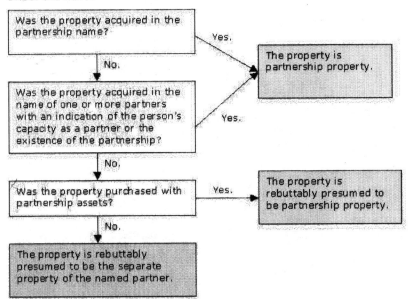

Comparison of a Partner's Property Rights
(generally same under UPA, RUPA, TRPA)

Agency & Partnership
SPARK LAW SERIES

In specific partnership property	In partnership interest
<ul><li>A partner has an equal right with co-partners to possess partnership property for partnership purposes</li><li>An individual partner has no right to assign partnership property</li><li>A partner's individual creditor may not attach partnership property</li><li>A partner's right in partnership property is not subject to family allowance</li></ul>	<ul><li>A partner has a right to share in the partnership's profits and surplus</li><li>A partner has a right to assign her partnership interest</li><li>A partner's individual creditor may obtain a charging order against the partner's interest in the partnership</li><li>A partner's interest in the partnership is subject to family allowance.</li></ul>

    C. Distributions on liquidation
        a. TRPA 1.01(2), 1.01(5), 4.01(a)-(b), 8.06
        b. RUPA §401(b)
        c. UPA §40(b)
        d. Note of Firm Financial Statements
            i. When a firm liquidates, it must settle its accounts and distribute its assets. It converts its assets into cash and uses the cash to pay its creditors. The firm then distributes whatever is left among its owners according to their rights.
            ii. 2 types of financial statements
                1. Balance Sheet
                2. Statement of Income
            iii. Balance Sheet
                1. Sets out the financial condition of a firm ON A SPECIFIC DATE
                2. Shows assets and equities
                3. Shows how the firm's assets would be distributed if the firm were liquidated on that date
                4. Equities: legal or equitable claims against the firm's assets
                    a. Two types

i. Liabilities
ii. Owners' Equity
b. Liabilities are amounts owed to creditors of the firm
c. Total liabilities is the aggregate amount that would be necessary to repay the firm's obligations to its creditors if the firm were liquidated as of the date of the balance sheet
d. Owner's equity represents the portion of the firm assets that would not be required to repay creditors, and is thus available for distribtution to the firm's owners

5. Equations:
$TotalAssets = TotalLiabilities + Owner'sEquity$
$Owner'sEquity = TotalAssets - TotalLiabilities$

6. Balance sheets are often presented in side by side columns
   a. Left column: firm assets
   b. Right column: liabilities and owner's equity
   c. The two columns must be total the same
   d. On liquidation, partners with net credits in their accounts are entitled to distributions, while those with net charges must make additional contributions

iv. Capital Account: a partner's account with the partnership
1. Includes both claims for contribution of capital and claims for profits

v. Statements of Income
1. Shows the result of a firm's operations over a specific period of time
2. Equation: *Income = Revenues – Expenses*
3. The words "earnings" or "profits" are used instead of "income" sometimes.

Agency & Partnership
SPARK LAW SERIES

4. Where a firm's revenues in a period exceed its expenses in that period, the firm has positive income.
5. Where a period's expenses exceed its revenues, the firm has negative income—it has incurred a loss for that period.

vi. Ex: Suppose a firm begins a period with Owner's Equity of $100,000, and has income of $100,000 during that period.
1. An income of $100,000 means that the firm's receipts of assets (revenues) exceed its expenditures of assets (expenses) by $100,000.
   a. Remember: Income = Revenues – Expenses
2. That is, the firm's total assets increased by $100,000.
3. All other things being equal, we would expect that Owner's Equity at the end of the period would increase by the same amount.
   a. Remember: Owner's Equity = Total Assets – Total Liabilities

D. Interim Distributions
   a. Delaware and Texas have the same approach as ULLCA for voting about distributions
   b. Delaware, Texas, and ULLCA are different on distributions (dividing up).
   c. ULLCA
      i. ULLCA §404(a)
      ii. ULLCA §404(c)
      iii. ULLCA §405(a)
      iv. ULLCA §406
      v. ULLCA §407
   d. Texas
      i. TLLCA §§ 2.12, 2.23, 5.02-1, 5.03, 5.04, 5.09
   e. Delaware
      i. Del LLC §§ 18-402, 504, 505, 503, 607
   f. *Brooke v. Mt. Hood Meadows:* Can the LP's compel the GP to distribute all profits?

i. Does the partnership agreement say that the LP's can mandate distributions? The agreement says that they're entitled to profits. What does that mean? It means that they can have the profits allocated to them, but they don't have to be actually paid out to them. The LP's own profits, but they may not be able to get to them all when they want. The agreement does not say they're entitled to distributions, just to allocations. That's an accounting matter.
ii. Same result under ULPA §15? The ULPA says "may" receive, not "shall" receive. But it also says "after such payment is made." What does that refer to? The share of the profits. So you could argue that the "such" clause shows that the profits need to be distributed.
iii. What if this were under UPA §18(a)? The partners would share equally in the profits.
iv. The court says that LPs don't have, by default under the statute, a contractual right to demand payments of 100% of the profits. Because it's a management decision that the general partners make. The GPs have discretion, but that discretion is still subject to fiduciary duties. It's not self-dealing when a GP decides to not distribute all profits... so good faith is not the inquiry... the business judgment rule is.
v. RUPA
1. RUPA §401(a)
vi. ULPA
1. ULPA §2
2. ULPA §7
3. ULPA §10(2)
4. ULPA §15
vii. RULPA
1. RULPA §503
2. RULPA §504
3. RULPA §601
E. Rights of Assignees and Creditors
a. Assignments
i. UPA §27
ii. RUPA §801(6)

iii. Problem 13.7
   1. Can you assign interests or profits? You cannot assign rights in specific property. You can assign your interests in the partnership. See UPA §26. See RUPA §503(1).
   2. What's the effect of dissolution? Does it dissolve the partnership? No.
   3. Is the assignee now a partner? No, they're just the transferee of the interest of the partner. The only way you can become a partner is with consent of all the partners (UPA §18(a)), unless the agreement says otherwise. Having an interest does not mean that the assignee can participate in management decisions; only partners can. Under the UPA and the RUPA, an assignee doesn't have a right to anything. An assignee doesn't have the right to inspect books. Texas allows the assignee the right to inspect books and records... nonuniform!
   4. So why would someone want to be a transferee? Because you're entitled to the profits the transferor would have been entitled to.
   5. You have another right, express under RUPA §503; UPA §27 doesn't say it; §28(2) says it; and 801(6) of the RUPA says a transferor may have a qualified right to go to court an ask for a judicial determination that is equitable to wind up the partnership needs.
   6. Suppose the partners decide they had been distributing money, but they don't want to anymore. Can the assignee sue the partners, not to force distributions, but can they sue for breach of fiduciary duty? Yes, if the partners made the decision in bad faith and not for a legitimate business purpose.

Agency & Partnership
SPARK LAW SERIES

       iv. You owe no fiduciary duties at all in connection with an assignee
- b. Charging Orders (and enforcing judgments)
    - i. UPA §28
    - ii. RUPA §504
    - iii. RUPA §503
    - iv. Lingo: under UPA... interest in partnership; RUPA... transferable interest in partnership; TX... partnership interest
    - v. Charging order is in some jurisdictions the exclusive remedy to get at an individual partner
    - vi. Texas: charging orders deleted from TRPA
    - vii. We know Connie can't get partnership property
    - viii. Connie can't get at Paula's right to partnership property
    - ix. Connie can't get at Paula's right to manage
    - x. Connie CAN get to interest in partnership... how would she do that?
        1. Get a charging order
        2. How to get a charging order:
            a. You have to be a judgment creditor (so if you're a general creditor, you have to get a judgment)
            b. Gotta get a court order
        3. Then what? Court can appoints receiver to get the distributions... and the receiver will receive the partner's interest until the lien is paid off.
        4. What's a charge: a lien on the debtor's transferable interest in the partnership
            a. So what does the lien get you? It means the court can foreclose on the debtor's interest.
            b. What does "debtor's interest" mean? Under UPA: Profits and surplus. Under RUPA: Share of Distributions.
        5. What happens if the court doesn't appoint a receiver? You'd have to notify the partnership that the partner's interest in the partnership is to be charged and direct

them until further notice, into the registry of the court, the interest due to the partners. The court will pay off the lien, and when it's paid off, the partnership will be notified that they can stop paying.
6. Why use a receiver at all? So that there's a better record of funds received. But there's a record if the court registry receives the funds.
7. What happens after the debt is paid? The charging order will be lifted and the partner is entitled to his distributions again.
8. What happens when the interest is foreclosed upon? The interest gets sold to a buyer, which means the money goes to the receiver who gives it to the judgment creditor to pay off the judgment.
    a. What happens if there's a balance due on the judgment? Who cares... it's of no concern of partnership law... that's creditor law.
    b. What happens if there's left over? It goes to the debtor-partner.
    c. How do you do a sale? Just like you would any other judicial sale.
    d. When the debt is gone, where do the distributions go? The transferee (purchaser) of the interest.
    e. Is the transferee now a partner? No.
    f. Is the debtor-partner still a partner? Yes. He retains his rights as normal, except to his interest in the partnership.
    g. What rights does the transferee have? The right to the distribution, if as and when they come. RUPA §503. But in Texas you also get the right to inspect the books.

                9. The debtor doesn't have to necessarily sell 100% of his interest… if his interest is worth substantially more than the debt.
                10. The court doesn't HAVE to order foreclosure.
            xi. A charging order is the statutory means by which a judgment creditor may reach the partnership interest of a judgment debtor
            xii. Common law procedures for collection: partnership property would be seized under writs of execution, the debtor partner's interest in the partnership would be sold subject to the payment of partnership debts and prior claims of the partnership against the debtor partner, and the sale of the debtor partner's interest would result in compulsory dissolution and winding up of the partnership
            xiii. Two collection methods
                1. Diversion of the debtor partner's profits to the judgment creditor
                2. The ultimate transfer of the debtor partner's interest (to be used if the first option didn't work)
            xiv. ULLCA §101(5) and (6)
            xv. RUPA §101(3)
            xvi. Conn LLC §34-171
            xvii. Conn UPA §34-66(1)
    c. Right to Dissolution
        i. UPA
            1. UPA §32
                a. Equivalent to RUPA §503(b)
            2. UPA §6(2)
            3. UPA §331(2)
        ii. RUPA
            1. RUPA §801(6)
            2. RUPA §806
            3. RUPA §101(8)
            4. RUPA §601
            5. RUPA §603
            6. RUPA §801
            7. RUPA §701
        iii. ULPA

Agency & Partnership
SPARK LAW SERIES

                1. ULPA §10(2), 16(2), 16(3), 19(3), 22, 9(1), 6(2)
        iv. RULPA
                1. RULPA §1105
                2. RULPA §802
                3. RULPA §602-04, 702-704, 902, 101(8), 101(10), 402-04,
        v. In effect, the charging order leaves the partnership intact but diverts to the judgment creditor the stream of profits that would otherwise flow to the debtor partner

METHODS OF TERMINATING AGENT'S AUTHORITY

ACTUAL AUTHORITY	APPARENT AUTHORITY
<ul><li>Expiration of agency term</li><li>Accomplishment of agency purpose</li><li>Destruction of subject matter or change of circumstances affecting value</li><li>Death or incapacity of principal or agent (except agencies coupled with an interest and durable powers of attorney)</li><li>By agreement or by act of one or both parties</li></ul>	<ul><li>Notification of termination to third parties (Parties with whom agent dealt usually must receive personal or individual notice; If apparent authority was created by public representation, public notice is generally required; If principal gave agent a written authority, principal must reclaim the writing or notify all parties with whom agent may deal. If the writing was recorded, the principal must record revocation.)</li><li>Death or incapacity of principal or agent</li></ul>

Dissociation of Non-Owners

A. Voluntary Terminations
   a. An agent can quit at any time for any reason
   b. A principal can fire an agent at any time for any reason

Agency & Partnership
SPARK LAW SERIES

    c.   **Notice that the Rest3d is non-uniform and so on test, unless it says to do so, use Rest2d, uniform rules, and common law rules**

    d.   Problem 14.1
- i. Does the former agent still have power to bind principal even if he no longer has actual authority?
- ii. Under what circumstances does the authority as with third parties stop?

    e.   Lingering apparent authority:
- i. An appearance of lingering authority
- ii. Sometimes continues power to bind, but only in limited circumstances
- iii. **Rest 3d §3.11(2):** apparent authority terminates when third party no longer can reasonably believe that the agent is authorized (i.e. that principal consents to be bound by the action)
    1. Shitty rule because it's not a very good basic principal
    2. "Reasonable belief" = ?????

    f.   Do all agents have lingering apparent authority?
- i. Under Rest 2d... general agent vs. special agent is relevant (know the difference between general and special agents)
- ii. **Rest2d §132 Test:** where the agent has not been held out as a general agent, the agent generally has no lingering apparent authority. A special agent will have lingering apparent authority only where (a) the principal has specially accredited the agent to the third person, (b) the principal has notice that the agent has begun to deal with the third person, OR (c) the principal has entrusted the agent with an indicia of authority.

    g.   Two types of termination
- i. Terminations by voluntary act
    1. "You're fired"
    2. "I quit"
- ii. Terminations by operation of law
    1. Death and loss of capacity

    h.   If an agent is in the middle of dealing with the third party, and the principal fires you, the third party must be notified of the termination (Rest2d§136(2)(c), p. 681)

Agency & Partnership
SPARK LAW SERIES

i. What's the only way to terminate when someone has indicia of authority, when it's unrealistic to give actual notice to everyone? Take it back... take back their keys. Take back the ID badge. Etc...
j. **Rest2d §127**: Ordinarily notice to a soliciting agent who countersigns and issues policies of insurance is notice to the insurance company.
k. A revocation of the agent's authority does not become effective as between the principal and third persons until they receive notice of the termination
l. **Rest2d §118**: The principal may at any time revoke his consent to action on his behalf by the agent
m. **Rest2d §119**: The authority of an agent to act for the principal terminates when the principal manifests to the agent that the principal no longer consents or when the agent has notice the principal no longer consents
n. **Rest2d §9(1) and §134**: The agent will have notice when the agent knows, has reason to know, should know, or has been given a notification of, the principal's lack of consent
o. **Rest2d §118, 119, 134**: An agent may renounce the agency and withdraw his consent to act on behalf of the principal. Authority terminates if the principal or the agent manifests to the other dissent to its continuance
p. **Rest2d §124A**: Termination of the agent's authority terminates all power of the agent to affect the principal's legal relations, except apparent authority and emergency authority
q. The extent of the agent's remaining apparent authority depends on the circumstances, including nature of the agency
r. **Rest2d §127**: a general agent continues to have apparent authority to bind the former principal to a third person despite a voluntary termination of the agency relationship until such time as the third person has notice of the termination
s. **Rest2d §135**: apparent authority continues until the third person (or the appropriate agent of the third person) knows, has reason to know, should know, or has been given a notification of the termination
t. **Rest2d §136(3)**: Notification by publication in a newspaper of general circulation in the place where the agency has regularly been carried on is effective to terminate the former

general agent's apparent authority as to all third persons except certain limited classes of persons

u. **Rest2d §136(2):** people entitled to actual notification... notification by publication is not effective where:
   i. The third person had previously extended or received credit to or from the principal through the general agent
   ii. The principal has specially accredited the agent to the third person
      1. Specially accredited: inviting a third person to deal with the agent
   iii. The principal should have known that the agent had already begun to deal with the third person
   iv. Where the principal has entrusted the agent with an indicia of authority
      1. Indicia of authority: a power of attorney or other writing given to the agent for the purpose of evidencing the agent's authority

v. **Rest2d §125:** while the agent has authority to bind the principal, third persons with notice of the principal's lack of consent can acquire no rights against the principal

w. Because the authority of an agent to act on behalf of the principal is based on the principal's consent for the agent so to act, the agent's authority to act sometimes terminates by implication. Implied terminations arise when the agent should realize that, in light of intervening events, the principal would no longer consent to action by the agent if the principal knew of the events.

x. The occurrence of the following events may call into question the continued consent of the principal
   i. A change in value of the subject matter of the agency or a change in business conditions (Rest2d §109)
   ii. The loss or destruction of the subject matter of the agency or the termination of the principal's inteRest2d in it (Rest2d §110)
   iii. A change of law of which the agent has notice and which causes the execution of his authority to be illegal, or which otherwise materially changes the effect of its execution (Rest2d §116)

Agency & Partnership
SPARK LAW SERIES

      iv. The bankruptcy or substantial impairment of the assets or credit of the agent or the principal of which the agent has notice (Rest2d §113, 114)

      v. The outbreak of war of which the agent has notice (Rest2d §115)

y. **Rest2d §124A:** the termination of authority does not thereby terminate apparent authority

z. **Rest3d §3.11(2):** Apparent authority ends when it is no longer reasonable for the third party with whom the agent deals to believe that the agent continues to act with actual authority. It is reasonable for third parties to assume that an agent's actual authority is a continuing or ongoing condition, unless and until the third party has notice of circumstances that make it unreasonable so to assume.

      i. Bad rule

      ii. Difference between Rest3d and Rest2d: no distinction between special and general agents: because the determination of whether a terminated agent may nevertheless bind the former principal is a fact question, whether the agent was a general or special agent may be relevant.

aa. Difference between Rest3d and Rest2d: termination of apparent authority.

      i. **Rest3d §3.11, comment e, Notice of termination of authority**: apparent authority is not present when a reasonable person in the position of a third party would not believe that the principal consents to the agent's or other actor's conduct. If a third party has notice of facts that call the agent's authority into question, and these facts would prompt a reasonable person to make inquiry of the principal before dealing with the agent, the agent does not act with apparent authority. This general principle is applicable to determining whether and when an agent acts with the lingering appearance of authority after the agent's actual authority has terminated. Lingering authority does not survive a statement that the agent's authority has terminated, made by the principal to the third party with whom the now-former agent deals. The principal's statement is effective even though the agent succeeds in persuading the third party to disregard it.

B. Terminations by Operation of Law
    a. Death
        i. Problem 14.3
            1. Death and loss of capacity terminates apparent authority by operation of law
            2. Common law rule: if someone dies that terminates the actual authority of an agent to act, because agency is a personal relationship. Cuts off actual authority without notice to the agent. Apparent authority is cut off without notification to the third party.
                a. Rejected by Rest3d, which said that apparent authority is not cut off until third party has reason to know of the death or incapacity; actual authority is not cut off until agent knows
        ii. Under the probate code, if someone become incapacitated, powers of attorney are generally cut off.
            1. A clause can be added that the power of attorney survives incapacity of the principal... this is what makes a power of attorney a durable power of attorney.
        iii. If agent did but the third party didn't know that the principal was dead, the principal is bound but the agent is subject to damages for breach of implied warranty of authority. You can disclaim your implied warranty of authority.
        iv. Public policy for apparent authority: it exists in order to allow third parties to depend on agents without investigating their agency before every single transaction.
        v. Reasonableness Test: an agent may take any action that he reasonably believes necessary to protect the

principal when the agent cannot communicate with the principal.
  vi. Because agency terminates at death, notice of a principal's death would make a reasonable person understand that the principal no longer consents to having the agent act for him.
  vii. **Rest2d §120 and 133:** (rejected by Rest3d) death terminates all power of the agent to bind the principal, both authority and apparent authority, without notice to either the agent or the third person dealing with the agent. Rationale: agency is a personal relation, necessarily ending with the death of the principal; the former principal is no longer a legal person with whom there can be legal relations. One cannot act on behalf of a non-existent person.
  viii. **Rest3d §3.07(2):** the death of an individual principal terminates the agent's actual authority. The termination is effective only when the agent has notice of the principal's death. The termination is also effective as against a third party with whom the agent deals when the party has notice of the principal's death.
  ix. **Rest3d §3.11 Termination of Apparent Authority:**
      1. The termination of actual authority does not by itself end any apparent authority held by the agent.
      2. Apparent authority ends when it is no longer reasonable for the third party with whom the agent deals to believe that the agent continues to act with actual authority.
b. Statutory Responses
  i. **Uniform Durable Power of Attorney Act §4:** the death or incapacity of a principal who has executed (any type, not just durable) written power of attorney does not revoke or terminate either (i) the authority of agent without knowledge of the principal's death or incapacity to act under the power of attorney, or (ii) the apparent authority of the agent as to third persons without knowledge of the principal's death or incapacity.

Agency & Partnership
SPARK LAW SERIES

  - ii. **Cal Civ Code §2356:** both authority and apparent authority continue until the agent and third person, respectively, know of the death or incapacity of the principal
  - iii. **Uniform Durable Power of Attorney Act §1:** A durable power of attorney is a written power of attorney that expressly provides that the power will not be affected by the subsequent disability or incapacity of the principal
  - iv. **Tex CPRC §135.001 to .018:** durable health care power of attorneys are authorized under which a person may appoint a health care agent to make such decisions on his behalf when he no longer has the capacity to make them
  - v. Living Will: a directive indicating his or her wishes regarding the continuance of medical treatment, life support, food, and water
- C. Irrevocable Agencies... **This power coupled with an interest topic is HARD! TWO DAYS SPENT ON THIS SECTION**
  - a. Problem
    - i. At common law, this is revocable because the subject matter is the ring and the fridge. If you take away the power to sell, does Dore have an interest in the fridge? No. He has an interest in the fridge to sell it to get money. So Dore's would not survive death under common law, but would under Rest.
    - ii. If they had a security agreement that included a clause that there was a power of attorney to sell the item on default, would there be an interest in the subject matter? Yes. So this would survive death under common law and under Rest.
    - iii. If you take away the power to sell, does Chase have an interest in the ring? Yes, because he has possession.
    - iv. Possession + Power to sell ≈ a lien
    - v. Under Rest, these are both powers given for consideration
  - b. Voluntary Terminations
    - i. Problem from website 14.4.5: this power of attorney cannot be revoked by voluntary act

Agency & Partnership
SPARK LAW SERIES

    ii. **Rest2d §118, cmt b:** the principal has power to revoke and the agent has power to renounce, although doing so is in violation of a contract between the parties and although the authority is expressed to be irrevocable.

    iii. Because the principal entrusts the agent with the power to bind him or her, the principal generally has the power to revoke at any time the agent's power to act on his or her behalf. Even where the principal and the agent have agreed that the agency would be irrevocable, or where the exercise of the power to revoke would otherwise violate a contract between the principal and the agent, the principal retains the power to revoke at will. The principal might well be liable in damages for revoking the agency in violation of the contract, but the principal nevertheless could revoke the agency.

    iv. Is a power of attorney, that's called "irrevocable" really irrevocable? Look to see if it fits into one of the categories below.

    v. The only agency powers that were irrevocable by voluntary act were
        1. Powers coupled with a separate interest in the subject matter of the power that arose independently of the agency power
            a. This will be irrevocable in all cases
            b. Ask: what is the interest? What is the subject matter? Is the interest in the subject matter? Is the interest independent of the power?
        2. Powers given for consideration or as security for the performance of a duty and given either at the time duty created or for later consideration (this is a Rest thing... not common law)

    vi. Rest2d vs. Common law: At common law only powers coupled with an interest survived the death of the principal. Although powers given for consideration or as security could not be revoked by voluntary act of the principal, such powers were

revoked by the death of the principal unless they were also coupled with an interest in the subject matter. In this area, the Rest2d tries to reform the law. See Rest2d §139.
vii. **Rest2d §138 Power given as security as a power defined**: a power created in the form of an agency authority, but held for the benefit of the power holder or a third person and given to secure the performance of a duty or to protect a title, either legal or equitable, such power being given when the duty or title is created or given for consideration.
viii. **Rest2d §139 Termination of Powers Given as Security:**
  1. Unless otherwise agreed, a power given as security is not terminated by
     a. Revocation by the creator of the power
     b. Surrender by the holder of the power, if he holds for the benefit of another
     c. The loss of capacity during the lifetime of either the creator of the power or the holder of the power, or
     d. The death of the holder of the power, or, if the power is given as security for a duty which does not terminate at the death of the creator of the power, by his death.
  2. A power given as security is terminated by its surrender by the beneficiary, if of full capacity; or by the happening of events which, by its terms, discharges the obligations secured by it, or which makes its execution illegal or impossible.
c. Terminations by Death of Principal
   i. **Rest3d§3.13(1)** powers given as security cannot be terminated by either a voluntary act of the principal or the principal's death. Instead a power given as security is terminated by an even that

1. Discharges the obligation secured by the power or terminates the interest secured or supported by proxy
2. Makes its execution illegal or impossible, or
3. Constitutes an effective surrender of the power or proxy by the person for whose benefit it was created or conferred.
    ii. **Rest3d §3.12(1):** a power given as security is a power to affect the legal relations of its creator that is created in the form of a manifestation of actual authority and held for the benefit of the holder or a third person. This power is given to protect a legal or equitable title, or to secure the performance of a duty apart from any duties owed the holder of the power by its creator that are incident to a relationship of agency under §1.01. It is given upon the creation of the duty or title or for consideration. It is distinct from actual authority that the holder may exercise if the holder is an agent of the creator of the power.
    iii. **Rest3d §3.12, comment b**: if the holder of a power given as security is not an agent, then the holder is not a fiduciary of the person who gave the power.
d. Other powers at common law:
    i. Power only given as security for (title or) performance of a duty (and not coupled with an interest)
        1. *at time duty or title created (and therefore the consideration is for the granting of the duty)
        2. *or if given later, for separate consideration
        3. This is a naked power and is irrevocable by voluntary act
        4. This is the Restatement view, which here is not the same as common law
        5. Common law view is that this **cannot** be revoked by voluntary act, but any termination of the power by operation of law revokes it unless it's also coupled with a separate interest in the subject matter of the power.

Agency & Partnership
SPARK LAW SERIES

      6. Common law says this creates an agency relationship
      7. Restatement says this is not an agency relationship, but that it looks like one. And while a person does have the ability to effect the legal stuff of someone, they're not acting as agents or fiduciaries because they're acting in their own commercial interest too
   e. Problem 14.5.5, if it shows up on test. Does it survive the death? The power of attorney does not survive the death, so the transfer is probably void on that grounds. Answer both issues.
   f. Rule: There is always power to revoke even if the revocation would be wrongful.
      i. Exceptions: unless the power to revoke is coupled with an interest.
   g. Recap: There are two ways of revoking an agency (1) voluntary act and (2) by operation of law {normally this is death}
   h. Rule: Power given for consideration, as security is irrevocable by voluntary act.
   i. So under the Common Law and the Restatement, this power of atty cannot be revoked by his voluntary act.

Power Coupled with an Interest
- For a power to be coupled with an interest:
  - The grantee's power (i.e. authority to bind, which appears like agency authority) must relate to some particular right or other property and
  - The same transaction that establishes the grantee's power must also provide the grantee some "interest" in that particular right or other property.
- For the power to be coupled with an interest, the power and the interest must relate to the same aspect of the particular property. If the grantee receives an interest not in the underlying property itself but rather in the proceeds that result from the grantee's exercise of granted power, then a true agency results and the grantee's authority is revocable.

Agency & Partnership
SPARK LAW SERIES

Authority (or power) Given as Security
- If
    - An obligor owes a debt or other obligation to an obligee, and
    - In order to provide the obligee with security, the obligor grants the obligee a power to bind the obligor,
- Then
    - No agency is created
    - The power is given as security and
    - The power is irrevocable during the life of the obligor

Sometimes circumstances will satisfy both concepts and a power given as security will also be a power coupled with an interest

Dissociation of Owners from Firms

A. Power to Withdraw or to Dissolve (In this section, we don't have to know anything that does not deal with plain-jane partnerships.)
   a. See chart handout
   b. Partnership at Will vs. Partnership for a definite term or a particular undertaking
      i. What do each of these mean under each code section?
      ii. Note: a general line of business is not a particular undertaking, it has to be capable of completion.
      iii. Sometimes courts will find an implied term or undertaking.
      iv. All of these can be dissolved at the will of a partner, but only a partnership-at-will will be rightly dissolved at the will of a partner
   c. Voluntary Dissolution: Partnerships at Wills
      i. UPA §29
      ii. UPA §30
      iii. UPA §31
         1. Read this section backwards
      iv. UPA §38(1)
         1. Says that where there's a rightful dissolution, each of the partners has the right to liquidation. They'll be paid in cash for the amount due to them.

Agency & Partnership
SPARK LAW SERIES

   2. "all persons claiming through them": this includes a transferee of the interest of the partnership, or something like that
   3. This section is a right of the partner, not of assignees
   4. "Unless otherwise agreed": the rights here can be contracted away
v. RUPA 601
   1. Dissociation ≠ Dissolution
   2. Note: §103(b) says you can't contract away the general right to withdraw.
   3. This is dissociation of the PARTNER
      a. Note under §801, dissolution and winding up of the PARTNERSHIP happens. This is not dissociation.
   4. §1 says the partner can withdraw at any time on notice. The only thing that can be contracted into is reasonable notice
vi. RUPA §603
   1. Does withdrawal necessarily result in dissociation? No. The partners can carry on the partnership.
      a. If it's carried on, technically the old partnership is wound up, and a new partnership is formed.
   2. See highlighted comment p. 38
vii. RUPA §801
RULPA §801 Non-judicial Dissolution: A limited partnership is dissolved and its affairs shall be wound up upon the happening of the first to occur: (1) at the time specified, (2) upon the happening of evens specified, (3) written consent of all partners, (4) an event of withdrawal of a GP unless there's another GP, but the LP is not dissolved if, within 90 days after the withdrawal, all partners agree in writing to continue the business of the limited partnership, and they appoint another GP.
   1. §1: causes dissolution if it's a partnership at will
   2. §101(8) defines dissolution

viii. Uniform/Majority rule: partnership at will is what? In a partnership at will, the partner has the right to get out, and that ends the partnership. You can contract away the winding up part, but not the right to get out
ix. Texas: defines partnership at will differently; and in a partnership at will, it takes a majority in interest vote to dissolve. If you withdraw, you're no longer a partner so you can't vote as to whether the partnership winds up, see 8.01(a). But if you use 8.01(g) and you just ask for a winding up, then if the majority-in-interest agree, then the partnership will be wound up.
x. Problem 15.1 (minus parts d and e, because they don't deal with regular partnerships)
  1. Attention brought to this problem, has been an exam question before
  2. This is a partnership at will, so under UPA §31(1)(b), it can be dissolved at any time by any partner without violating the partnership agreement
  3. (part a): What is the effect of Maria writing a letter saying she quits?
     a. Under UPA, the partnership is dissolved
     b. Test for dissolution: §29
     c. Dissolution is a change in lifestyle. Upon dissolution, the partnership is not to start any new business. It only exists so that it can finish up the business. Then the partnership is dissolved.
     d. "ceasing to be associated"
     e. The entire partnership is affected; the partnership continues but only for the purpose of winding up.
     f. What causes dissolution? UPA §31.
     g. Is Maria violating the partnership agreement?

Agency & Partnership
SPARK LAW SERIES

- h. Can the partners vote as to whether or not to continue the partnership or to wind up? No... voting is only for ordinary business.
    - i. UPA §38(1) applies
    - ii. Can Maria insist on liquidation? Yes.
    - iii. What could have been done to avoid this result? If they would have agreed. They could agree in advance, or they could agree now.
    - iv. Why is this the default rule? Because partners are personally obligated on partnership liabilities and liquidation gives them a way to have closure and walk away free.
        - i. Same result under RUPA?
- xi. UPA §31(1)(b) and §38(1)(1st sentence): Partnership at will
- xii. Remember: a partner has a right to withdraw as a partner, which automatically triggers winding up

d. Voluntary Dissolution: Partnerships Not at Will
   i. Problem 15.2
   1. Attention brought to this problem, has been an exam question before
   2. Suppose the partnership agreement provided for a 10-year term. And after 5 years, and Maria decides to leave
   3. Agreeing to remain a partner for 10 years makes them a partnership for a definite term or undertaking
   4. Can Maria still leave even if it's not been 10 years yet?
   5. UPA §31(1)(a) says that if a partnership not at will, there is no violation of the agreement for the partnership to end at the end of the agreement

Agency & Partnership
SPARK LAW SERIES

6. Both §31(1) and (2) are voluntary causes of dissolution, as opposed to dissolutions by operation by law
7. UPA §31(2) is what Maria will use... and it is a violation of the agreement. Any partner has the right to get out, but if you're not causing dissolution under §31(1) then you are in breach of the partnership agreement.
8. Does the first sentence of §38(1) apply? No, because this is applicable when there is not contravention of the partnership agreement.
9. So you go to §38(2)... which applies when there is a §31 breach
    a. (a) applies to the partners who didn't cause dissolution wrongfully
    b. (b) applies to the partners who didn't cause dissolution wrongfully
    c. Here, "dissolution wrongfully" means not in contravention of the agreement
    d. Under (a)(1) they have the rights in paragraph 1: the right to insist upon liquidation (the liquidation right), and (2) a right to damages against the breaching partner for breach of the agreement, and they have (b) the right to continue the business (note: they are continuing the business, but not the partnership), they can continue for the remainder of the agreed term, and they all have to agree.
    e. Note: only partners may possess partnership property, but this section says that can continue to use partnership property, even though they aren't a partnership anymore, as long as (1) they pay the breaching partner the value of his interest (minus damages for

breach of the agreement) and (2) they have to indemnify the wrongful against all present and future partnership agreements
      i. Won't need to know the bond with the court stuff
f. (c) lists the rights of the breaching partner
      i. (I) A qualified liquidation right if the others do not elect to continue, subject to damages
      ii. (II) right to the value of the interest in cash minus damages
          1. Note: the last three lines...the value of the goodwill of the business will not be considered in calculating the value of his interest. Calculate his value using tangible assets only. Ignore future earning potential (called goodwill), which is an asset.
          2. **NOTE: Major change in RUPA... which does not deduct this from your interest... You get the full value of your interest**
      iii. And under II, he also has the right to be released from all existing partnership agreements.
      iv. What are the only two ways to release someone from an obligation? (1)

Agency & Partnership
SPARK LAW SERIES

        fulfilling it (here, paying off partnership creditors) or (2) get each and every creditor to release the partner that's leaving.
        1. **UPA ONLY**
        2. This requirement can be contracted around, so the partnership agreement can provide that in the event of an early termination, they don't have to be released.

Note: this is common

Note: there is a risk here... the only time a creditor will come after you is when the partnership has exhausted all the assets. And if there's nothing left in the partnership and there are still debts, then what good is your indemnification?

      g. ...Summarize this crud
   ii. On Problem 15.2(b), under the RUPA... that is not an agreement that the partnership will last for a certain term, it's just an agreement that no one will leave early.
      a. Note: courts will sometimes imply a term
   iii. Problem 15.2(c), under UPA, such an agreement isn't worth anyway, she can still leave, she can still liquidate, she is entitled to full value of interest... but will be liable for damages for breach under contract law
   iv. Same argument under RUPA in 15.2(b) and (c)
   v. Note, in Texas...
      1. 6.01(b)(1), you can't contract away you right to withdraw (this is actually in all the codes)

2. The difference between B and C, dissolution by a majority vote is the same as a partnership that dissolves that the occurrence of a particular event
vi. Under RUPA, the structure is different, but has almost the same result.
   1. Make sure to know all these little differences
   2. Distinguishes between a partner leaving and dissolution of the partnership that requires winding up
      a. Note, a 601(1) withdrawal automatically triggers a 801 winding up
      b. Under 801, has dissolution been triggered when a partner withdraws?
         i. Note, not under 801(1) which is for partnership at will
      c. See highlighted comment p. 43
   3. 801(2)(i) this is a major variation from the UPA. Under RUPA, at least half can agree to windup
   4. Do we have a wrongful dissociation? §602(b) tells us when it's wrongful
      a. §602(b)(2)(i) Nina can withdraw and doesn't commit a wrongful act, but doesn't not have the right to insist upon liquidation
         i. don't need to know (ii) to (iv)
   5. For 15.2(b) and (c), §502(b)(1), if a partner agree to something and one of them doesn't follow it, the dissociation is wrongful... but it's still a partnership at will (so there's a dissolution under §801(1))
      a. Note: 802(b), not all the partners get to vote... the breaching partner doesn't get to. Maria doesn't get to vote even though it's a

Agency & Partnership
SPARK LAW SERIES

     partnership at will. SO Nina and Pinta can continue
      i. But... under 15.2(c) says it takes all of them
    6. The difference in Texas: you have an express occurrence, so it's not a partnership at will in Texas... so you're under 6.02(b)(2)
  e. ***Canter's Pharmacy v. Elizabeth Associates***
    i. What does particular undertaking mean? A particular undertaking must be capable of accomplishment at some time, although the exact time may be unknown and unascertainable at the date of the agreement.
     1. Leasing property involved entering into a business relationship which may continue indefinitely; there is nothing particular about it.
    ii. In certain circumstances a partnership may be dissolvable by the express will of any partner at any time.
    iii. If no definite term or particular undertaking is specified in the partnership agreement, at-will dissolution does not violate the agreement between the partners. An expression of a will to dissolve is effective as a dissolution even if in contravention of the agreement.
    iv. One cannot be coerced to remain in a partnership against his or her wishes.
    v. The dissolution of a partnership does not mean that the partnership ceases doing business
    vi. Termination of a partnership is markedly different from the dissolution of a partnership. When a partnership has terminated it ceases doing business; when a partner effects a dissolution it simply means that partner is no longer associated with the business of the partnership.
  f. RUPA §101(8)
  g. Because partners are liable for partnership obligations, allowing them to dissolve even a partnership for a term or undertaking allows them to avoid additional liability on new partnership obligations.

- h. Partners must notify third persons that they are no longer associated with the business.
- i. Note on Withdrawal and Dissolution in Partnerships
    - i. UPA
        1. Right to Liquidation
            - a. Each partner generally has the right to have partnership affairs wound up.
            - b. Winding up involves:
                - i. Completion of unfinished partnership business
                - ii. The liquidation of partnership property and the discharge of partnership obligations
                - iii. Settlement of partnership accounts
                - iv. The payment in cash of the net amount due each partner
        2. Right to continue partnership business (UPA §38(2))
            - a. A partner loses the right to liquidation when the partner has caused dissolution wrongfully or in contravention of the partnership agreement
            - b. A partner wrongfully causes dissolution when the partner voluntarily dissolves the partnership before the completion of an agreed definite term or particular undertaking
            - c. Where the partners have not agreed to a definite term or particular undertaking, any partner may by express will dissolve the partnership without violation of the agreement between the partners

d. Dissolution by express will is wrongful only when it occurs before the completion of an agreed definite term or particular undertaking. The other partners can continue the partnership business only for the remainder of the agreed term of the partnership.
e. Unless the partnership agreement provides otherwise, the consent of all the other ("innocent") partners is required before the business can be continued under the UPA. That is, each of the innocent partners has the right to liquidation.
f. If the innocent partners elect to continue the partnership business, the partner wrongfully causing dissolution loses the right to liquidation. Instead, the partner wrongfully causing dissolution is only entitled to be paid the value of the partner's interest in the partnership, but without including any value for goodwill of the partnership business and less any damages.
g. In addition, the partner wrongfully causing dissolution must be released from existing liabilities of the partnership

3. Continuation of Business, not Continuation of Partnership
    a. Any change in partner composition technically works a dissolution of the existing partnership. Where the partners continue the business without winding up partnership affairs, they do so as a new, different partnership

ii. RUPA
   1. Dissociation and Dissolution
      a. Dissociation and Dissolution are different
      b. When a partner dissociates from the partnership, that partner is no longer associated in the carrying on of business by the partnership.
      c. Where the remaining partners are permitted to continue doing business without a winding up, there is no reason why they should not be viewed as continuing their association with each other. (Legal terms: although one partner is no longer associated with the carrying on of business by the partnership entity, the partnership entity continues despite the dissociation)
      d. Dissolution occurs only on the occurrence of an event that requires the winding up of the partnership business
   2. Unqualified Power to Dissociate
      a. Partners have an unqualified power to dissociate from a partnership—to withdraw by express will.
      b. A partner may dissociate even though that withdrawal is wrongful as to the other partners.
      c. Partners may not contract away their power to dissociate, except to require written notice.
   3. Power to Dissolve—Partnerships at Will
      a. A partner's withdrawal by express will dissolves the partnership.
      b. Unlike the power to dissociate, a partner may contract away the power to dissolve a partnership at will.

c. Any time before winding up of the partnership business is complete, all the partners may waive the right to have the partnership's business wound up.
4. Continuation after an Early Dissociation from a Partnership for a Definite Term or a Particular Undertaking
    a. No single partner has the power to dissolve the partnership before the expiration of the term or the completion of the undertaking.
    b. Each partner retains the power to dissociate by express will at any time, but any withdrawal before the expiration of the definite term or the completion of the specific undertaking would generally be wrongful.
    c. The partnership is not dissolved after an early withdrawal, except upon the express will of at least half of the other partners.
    d. On the other hand, any of the other partners may rightfully withdraw form the partnership after another partner's wrongful dissociation, bankruptcy, or death.
    e. When there is no dissolution of the partnership, the partnership must purchase the withdrawing partner's interest in the partnership. The partnership must also indemnify the withdrawing partner against partnership liabilities.
5. Wrongful Dissociation
    a. A partner's dissociation is wrongful only if:

                i. The dissociation violates the partnership agreement, or
                ii. Before the expiration of a definite term or the completion of a specific undertaking, a partner dissociates by express will, is judicially expelled, becomes bankrupt, or (if a legal entity and not a natural person) willfully dissolves or terminates.
            b. The chief consequence of a wrongful dissociation is that the wrongful dissociating partner is liable for damages.
            c. In addition, partners who wrongfully dissociate before the expiration of a definite term or specific undertaking are not entitled to payment for the partner's interest in the partnership until the expiration of the term or the completion of the undertaking.
    6. Withdrawal
        a. Similar to RUPA
        b. Partners have the power to withdraw at any time and that power may not be contracted away
        c. A partner's withdrawal is wrongful if:
            i. It breaches the partnership agreement or
            ii. Where the partner has withdrawn prior to:
                1. The expiration of any agreed definite term,

2. The completion of an agreed particular undertaking, or
3. The occurrence of an agreed specified event.
7. Winding Up
   a. Unless the partnership agreement provides otherwise, where there is no definite term, particular undertaking, or specified event upon which the partnership is to be wound up:
      i. A majority-in-interest of the partners may voluntarily dissolve the partnership
      ii. A partner who has not agreed not to withdraw may request a winding up of the partnership, but the partnership will not be wound up if a majority-in-interest of the partners agree to continue the partnership.
   b. Where a partner withdraws, and the partnership is not required to be wound up, the partnership must purchase the interest of the withdrawing partner.

CAUSES OF DISSOLUTION UNDER THE UPA

Acts of the Partners	Operation of Law	Decree of Court
<ul><li>Per partnership agreement</li><li>By will of partner</li><li>Mutual assent of partners</li><li>Expulsion of partner</li></ul>	<ul><li>Illegality</li><li>Death of partner</li><li>Bankruptcy of partner</li></ul>	<ul><li>Incompetency of partner</li><li>Incapability of partner</li><li>Improper conduct of partner</li><li>Business operating only at a loss</li><li>Circumstances rendering dissolution equitable</li></ul>

APPROACH TO ORDER OF DISTRIBUTION OF ASSETS UNDER THE UPA

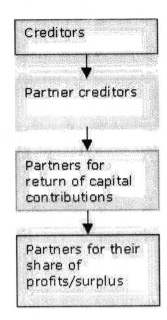

Agency & Partnership
SPARK LAW SERIES

TABLE OF CASES

Bancroft-Whitney Co. v. Glen 29, 44
Bane v. Ferguson 44
Billops v. Magness Construction Co. 13
Fenwick v. Unemployment Compensation Commission 40
General Automotive Mfg. Co. v. Singer 28
Hoover v. Sun Oil Company 9
Humble Oil & Refining Co. v. Martin 9
Kidd v. Thomas A. Edison, Inc. 23
Lind v. Schenley Industries, Inc. 20
Meehan v. Shaughnessy 43
Meinhard v. Salmon 43
Mill Street Church of Christ v. Hogan 19
Murphy v. Holiday Inns, Inc. 10
National Biscuit Company v. Stroud 45
Nogales Service Center v. Atlantic Richfield Co. 24
Owen v. Cohen 52
Parker v. Domino's Pizza 10
Watteau v. Fenwick 23

Agency & Partnership
SPARK LAW SERIES

APPENDIX

UNIFORM PARTNERSHIP ACT (1914)

§ 6. Partnership Defined

(1) A partnership is an association of two or more persons to carry on as co-owners a business for profit.

§ 7. Rules for Determining the Existence of a Partnership

In determining whether a partnership exists, these rules shall apply:

(1) . . .

(2) Joint tenancy, tenancy in common, tenancy by the entireties, joint property, common property, or part ownership does not of itself establish a partnership, whether such co-owners do or do not share any profits made by the use of the property.

(3) The sharing of gross returns does not of itself establish a partnership, whether or not the persons sharing them have a joint or common right or interest in any property from which the returns are derived.

(4) The receipt by a person of a share of the profits of a business is prima facie evidence that he is a partner in the business, but no such inference shall be drawn if such profits were received in payment:

>(a) As a debt by installments or otherwise,
>(b) As wages of an employee or rent to a landlord,
>(c) . . .
>(d) As interest on a loan, though the amount of payment vary with the profits of the business,
>(e) . . .

Agency & Partnership
SPARK LAW SERIES

§ 8. Partnership Property

(1) All property originally brought into the partnership stock or subsequently acquired by purchase or otherwise, on account of the partnership, is partnership property.

(2) Unless the contrary intention appears, property acquired with partnership funds is partnership property.

§ 9. Partner Agent of Partnership as to Partnership Business

(1) Every partner is an agent of the partnership for the purpose of its business, and the act of every partner, including the execution in the partnership name of any instrument, for apparently carrying on in the usual way the business of the partnership of which he is a member binds the partnership, unless the partner so acting has in fact no authority to act for the partnership in the particular matter, and the person with whom he is dealing has knowledge of the fact that he has no such authority.

(2) An act of a partner which is not apparently for the carrying on of the business of the partnership in the usual way does not bind the partnership unless authorized by the other partners.

(3) Unless authorized by the other partners or unless they have abandoned the business, one or more but less than all the partners have no authority to:

(a) Assign the partnership property in trust for creditors or on the assignee's promise to pay the debts of the partnership,

(b) . . .

(c) Do any other act which would make it impossible to carry on the ordinary business of a partnership,

(d) . . .

(e) . . .

(4) No act of a partner in contravention of a restriction on authority shall bind the partnership to persons having knowledge of the restriction.

§ 11. Partnership Bound by Admission of Partner

An admission or representation made by any partner concerning partnership affairs within the scope of his authority as conferred by this act is evidence against the partnership.

§ 12. Partnership Charged with Knowledge of or Notice to Partner

Notice to any partner of any matter relating to partnership affairs, and the knowledge of the partner acting in the particular matter, acquired while a partner or then present to his mind, and the knowledge of any other partner who reasonably could and should have communicated it to the acting partner, operate as notice to or knowledge of the partnership, except in the case of a fraud on the partnership committed by or with the consent of that partner.

§ 13. Partnership Bound by Partner's Wrongful Act

Where, by any wrongful act or omission of any partner acting in the ordinary course of the business of the partnership or with the authority of his co-partners, loss or injury is caused to any person, not being a partner in the partnership, or any penalty is incurred, the partnership is liable therefore to the same extent as the partner so acting or omitting to act.

§ 14. Partnership Bound by Partner's Breach of Trust

The partnership is bound to make good the loss:

(a) Where one partner acting within the scope of his apparent authority receives money or property of a third person and misapplies it; and

(b) Where the partnership in the course of its business receives money or property of a third person and the money or property so received is misapplied by any partner while it is in the custody of the partnership

§ 15. Nature of Partner's Liability

All partners are liable

(a) Jointly and severally for everything chargeable to the partnership under sections 13 and 14 [wrongful acts and breaches of trust].

(b) Jointly for all other debts and obligations of the partnership; but any partner may enter into a separate obligation to perform a partnership contract.

§ 18. Rules Determining Rights and Duties of Partners

The rights and duties of the partners in relation to the partnership shall be determined, subject to any agreement between them, by the following rules:

(a) Each partner shall be repaid his contributions . . . and share equally in the profits and surplus remaining after all liabilities, including those to partners, are satisfied; and must contribute towards the losses, whether of capital or otherwise, sustained by the partnership according to his share in the profits.

(b) The partnership must indemnify every partner in respect of payments made and personal liabilities reasonably incurred by him in the ordinary and proper conduct of its business, or for the preservation of its business or property.

(c) . . .
(d) . . .

(e) All partners have equal rights in the management and conduct of the partnership business.

(f) . . .

(g) No person can become a member of a partnership without the consent of all the partners.

(h) Any difference arising as to ordinary matters connected with the partnership business may be decided by a majority of the partners; but no act in contravention of any agreement between the partners may be done rightfully without the consent of all the partners.

§ 21. Partner Accountable as a Fiduciary

(1) Every partner must account to the partnership for any benefit, and hold as trustee for it any profits derived by him without the consent of the other partners from any transaction connected with the formation, conduct, or liquidation of the partnership or from any use by him of its property.

§ 29. Dissolution Defined

The dissolution of a partnership is the change in the relation of the partners caused by any partner ceasing to be associated in the carrying on as distinguished from the winding up of the business.

§ 30. Partnership not Terminated by Dissolution

On dissolution the partnership is not terminated, but continues until the winding up of partnership affairs is completed.

§ 31. Causes of Dissolution

Dissolution is caused:
(1) Without violation of the agreement between the partners,

    (a) By the termination of the definite term or particular undertaking specified in the agreement,

    (b) By the express will of any partner when no definite term or particular undertaking is specified,

(c) By the express will of all the partners who have not assigned their interests or suffered them to be charged for their separate debts, either before or after the termination of any specified term or particular undertaking,

(d) By the expulsion of any partner from the business bona fide in accordance with such a power conferred by the agreement between the partners;

(2) In contravention of the agreement between the partners, where the circumstances do not permit a dissolution under any other provision of this section, by the express will of any partner at any time;

(3) By any event which makes it unlawful for the business of the partnership to be carried on or for the members to carry it on in partnership;

(4) By the death of any partner;

(5) By the bankruptcy of any partner or the partnership;

(6) By decree of court . . .

§ 32. Dissolution by Decree of Court

(1) On application by or for a partner the court shall decree a dissolution whenever:

(a) A partner has been declared a lunatic in any judicial proceeding or is shown to be of unsound mind,

(b) A partner becomes in any other way incapable of performing his part of the partnership contract,

(c) A partner has been guilty of such conduct as tends to affect prejudicially the carrying on of the business,

(d) A partner wilfully or persistently commits a breach of the partnership agreement, or otherwise so conducts himself in matters relating to the partnership business that it is not reasonably practicable to carry on the business in partnership with him,

(e) The business of the partnership can only be carried on at a loss,

(f) Other circumstances render a dissolution equitable.

(2) On the application of the purchaser of a partner's interest under sections 28 or 29: [FN1]

(a) After the termination of the specified term or particular undertaking,

(b) At any time if the partnership was a partnership at will when the interest was assigned or when the charging order was issued.

Agency & Partnership
SPARK LAW SERIES

REVISED UNIFORM PARTNERSHIP ACT (1997)

ARTICLE 1. GENERAL PROVISIONS

§ 101. Definitions

In this [Act]:

(1) "Business" includes every trade, occupation, and profession.

(2) . . .
(3) . . .
(4) . . .
(5) "Limited liability partnership" means a partnership that has filed a statement of qualification under Section 1001 and does not have a similar statement in effect in any other jurisdiction.

(6) "Partnership" means an association of two or more persons to carry on as co-owners a business for profit formed under Section 202, predecessor law, or comparable law of another jurisdiction.

(7) "Partnership agreement" means the agreement, whether written, oral, or implied, among the partners concerning the partnership, including amendments to the partnership agreement.

(8) "Partnership at will" means a partnership in which the partners have not agreed to remain partners until the expiration of a definite term or the completion of a particular undertaking.

§ 103. Effect of Partnership Agreement; Non-waivable Provisions

(a) Except as otherwise provided in subsection (b), relations among the partners and between the partners and the partnership are governed by the partnership agreement. To the extent the partnership agreement does not otherwise provide, this [Act] governs relations among the partners and between the partners and the partnership.

(b) The partnership agreement may not:

Agency & Partnership
SPARK LAW SERIES

(1) vary the rights and duties under Section 105 except to eliminate the duty to provide copies of statements to all of the partners;

(2) unreasonably restrict the right of access to books and records under Section 403(b);

(3) eliminate the duty of loyalty...

(4) unreasonably reduce the duty of care...;

(5) eliminate the obligation of good faith and fair dealing)...;

(6) vary the power to dissociate...;

(7) vary the right of a court to expel a partner in the events specified in Section 601(5);

(8) vary the requirement to wind up the partnership business in cases specified in Section 801(4), (5), or (6);

(9) vary the law applicable to a limited liability partnership under Section 106(b); or

(10) restrict rights of third parties under this [Act].

ARTICLE 2. NATURE OF THE PARTNERSHIP

§ 201. Partnership as Entity

(a) A partnership is an entity distinct from its partners.

§ 202. Formation of Partnership

(a) Except as otherwise provided in subsection (b), the association of two or more persons to carry on as co-owners a business for profit forms a partnership, whether or not the persons intend to form a partnership.

Agency & Partnership
SPARK LAW SERIES

§ 203. Partnership Property

   Property acquired by a partnership is property of the partnership and not of the partners individually.

ARTICLE 3. RELATIONS OF PARTNERS TO PERSONS DEALING WITH PARTNERSHIP

§ 301. Partner Agent of Partnership

   Subject to the effect of a statement of partnership authority under Section 303:

   (1) Each partner is an agent of the partnership for the purpose of its business. An act of a partner, including the execution of an instrument in the partnership name, for apparently carrying on in the ordinary course the partnership business or business of the kind carried on by the partnership binds the partnership, unless the partner had no authority to act for the partnership in the particular matter and the person with whom the partner was dealing knew or had received a notification that the partner lacked authority.

   (2) An act of a partner which is not apparently for carrying on in the ordinary course the partnership business or business of the kind carried on by the partnership binds the partnership only if the act was authorized by the other partners.

§ 305. Partnership Liable for Partner's Actionable Conduct

   (a) A partnership is liable for loss or injury caused to a person, or for a penalty incurred, as a result of a wrongful act or omission, or other actionable conduct, of a partner acting in the ordinary course of business of the partnership or with authority of the partnership.

   (b) If, in the course of the partnership's business or while acting with authority of the partnership, a partner receives or causes the partnership to receive money or property of a person not a partner, and the money or property is misapplied by a partner, the partnership is liable for the loss.

§ 306. Partner's Liability

(a) Except as otherwise provided in subsections (b) and (c), all partners are liable jointly and severally for all obligations of the partnership unless otherwise agreed by the claimant or provided by law.

(b) A person admitted as a partner into an existing partnership is not personally liable for any partnership obligation incurred before the person's admission as a partner.

(c) An obligation of a partnership incurred while the partnership is a limited liability partnership, whether arising in contract, tort, or otherwise, is solely the obligation of the partnership. A partner is not personally liable, directly or indirectly, by way of contribution or otherwise, for such an obligation solely by reason of being or so acting as a partner. This subsection applies notwithstanding anything inconsistent in the partnership agreement that existed immediately before the vote required to become a limited liability partnership under Section 1001(b).

§ 307. Actions By and Against Partnership and Partners

(a) A partnership may sue and be sued in the name of the partnership.

(b) An action may be brought against the partnership and, to the extent not inconsistent with Section 306, any or all of the partners in the same action or in separate actions.

(c) A judgment against a partnership is not by itself a judgment against a partner. A judgment against a partnership may not be satisfied from a partner's assets unless there is also a judgment against the partner.

(d) A judgment creditor of a partner may not levy execution against the assets of the partner to satisfy a judgment based on a claim against the partnership unless the partner is personally liable for the claim under Section 306 and:

(1) a judgment based on the same claim has been obtained against the partnership and a writ of execution on the judgment has been returned unsatisfied in whole or in part;

(2) the partnership is a debtor in bankruptcy;

(3) the partner has agreed that the creditor need not exhaust partnership assets;

(4) a court grants permission to the judgment creditor to levy execution against the assets of a partner based on a finding that partnership assets subject to execution are clearly insufficient to satisfy the judgment, that exhaustion of partnership assets is excessively burdensome, or that the grant of permission is an appropriate exercise of the court's equitable powers; or

(5) liability is imposed on the partner by law or contract independent of the existence of the partnership.

ARTICLE 4. RELATIONS OF PARTNERS TO EACH OTHER AND TO PARTNERSHIP

§ 401. Partners' Rights and Duties

(a) Each partner is deemed to have an account that is:

(1) credited with an amount equal to the money plus the value of any other property, net of the amount of any liabilities, the partner contributes to the partnership and the partner's share of the partnership profits; and

(2) charged with an amount equal to the money plus the value of any other property, net of the amount of any liabilities, distributed by the partnership to the partner and the partner's share of the partnership losses.

(b) Each partner is entitled to an equal share of the partnership profits and is chargeable with a share of the partnership losses in proportion to the partner's share of the profits.

(c) A partnership shall reimburse a partner for payments made and indemnify a partner for liabilities incurred by the partner in the ordinary course of the business of the partnership or for the preservation of its business or property.

(d) A partnership shall reimburse a partner for an advance to the partnership beyond the amount of capital the partner agreed to contribute.

(e) A payment or advance made by a partner which gives rise to a partnership obligation under subsection (c) or (d) constitutes a loan to the partnership which accrues interest from the date of the payment or advance.

(f) Each partner has equal rights in the management and conduct of the partnership business.

(g) A partner may use or possess partnership property only on behalf of the partnership.

(h) A partner is not entitled to remuneration for services performed for the partnership, except for reasonable compensation for services rendered in winding up the business of the partnership.

(i) A person may become a partner only with the consent of all of the partners.

(j) A difference arising as to a matter in the ordinary course of business of a partnership may be decided by a majority of the partners. An act outside the ordinary course of business of a partnership and an amendment to the partnership agreement may be undertaken only with the consent of all of the partners.

(k) This section does not affect the obligations of a partnership to other persons under Section 301.

§ 404. General Standards of Partner's Conduct

(a) The only fiduciary duties a partner owes to the partnership and the other partners are the duty of loyalty and the duty of care set forth in subsections (b) and (c).

(b) A partner's duty of loyalty to the partnership and the other partners is limited to the following:

(1) to account to the partnership and hold as trustee for it any property, profit, or benefit derived by the partner in the conduct and winding up of the partnership business or derived from a use by the partner of partnership property, including the appropriation of a partnership opportunity;

(2) to refrain from dealing with the partnership in the conduct or winding up of the partnership business as or on behalf of a party having an interest adverse to the partnership; and

(3) to refrain from competing with the partnership in the conduct of the partnership business before the dissolution of the partnership.

(c) A partner's duty of care to the partnership and the other partners in the conduct and winding up of the partnership business is limited to refraining from engaging in grossly negligent or reckless conduct, intentional misconduct, or a knowing violation of law.

(d) A partner shall discharge the duties to the partnership and the other partners under this [Act] or under the partnership agreement and exercise any rights consistently with the obligation of good faith and fair dealing.

(e) A partner does not violate a duty or obligation under this [Act] or under the partnership agreement merely because the partner's conduct furthers the partner's own interest.

Agency & Partnership
SPARK LAW SERIES

ARTICLE 6. PARTNER'S DISSOCIATION

§ 601. Events Causing Partner's Dissociation

A partner is dissociated from a partnership upon the occurrence of any of the following events:

(1) the partnership's having notice of the partner's express will to withdraw as a partner or on a later date specified by the partner;

(2) an event agreed to in the partnership agreement as causing the partner's dissociation;

(3) the partner's expulsion pursuant to the partnership agreement;

(4) the partner's expulsion by the unanimous vote of the other partners if:

(i) it is unlawful to carry on the partnership business with that partner;

(ii) there has been a transfer of all or substantially all of that partner's transferable interest in the partnership, other than a transfer for security purposes, or a court order charging the partner's interest, which has not been foreclosed;

(iii) within 90 days after the partnership notifies a corporate partner that it will be expelled because it has filed a certificate of dissolution or the equivalent, its charter has been revoked, or its right to conduct business has been suspended by the jurisdiction of its incorporation, there is no revocation of the certificate of dissolution or no reinstatement of its charter or its right to conduct business; or

(iv) a partnership that is a partner has been dissolved and its business is being wound up;

(5) on application by the partnership or another partner, the partner's expulsion by judicial determination because:

(i) the partner engaged in wrongful conduct that adversely and materially affected the partnership business;

(ii) the partner willfully or persistently committed a material breach of the partnership agreement or of a duty owed to the partnership or the other partners under Section 404; or

(iii) the partner engaged in conduct relating to the partnership business which makes it not reasonably practicable to carry on the business in partnership with the partner.

(6) the partner's:

(i) becoming a debtor in bankruptcy;

(ii) executing an assignment for the benefit of creditors;

(iii) seeking, consenting to, or acquiescing in the appointment of a trustee, receiver, or liquidator of that partner or of all or substantially all of that partner's property; or

(iv) failing, within 90 days after the appointment, to have vacated or stayed the appointment of a trustee, receiver, or liquidator of the partner or of all or substantially all of the partner's property obtained without the partner's consent or acquiescence, or failing within 90 days after the expiration of a stay to have the appointment vacated.

(7) in the case of a partner who is an individual:

(i) the partner's death;

(ii) the appointment of a guardian or general conservator for the partner; or

(iii) a judicial determination that the partner has otherwise become incapable of performing the partner's duties under the partnership agreement;

Agency & Partnership
SPARK LAW SERIES

§ 602. Partner's Power to Dissociate; Wrongful Dissociation

(a) A partner has the power to dissociate at any time, rightfully or wrongfully, by express will pursuant to Section 601(1).

(b) A partner's dissociation is wrongful only if:

(1) it is in breach of an express provision of the partnership agreement; or

(2) in the case of a partnership for a definite term or particular undertaking, before the expiration of the term or the completion of the undertaking:

(i) the partner withdraws by express will, unless the withdrawal follows within 90 days after another partner's dissociation by death or otherwise under Section 601(6) through (10) or wrongful dissociation under this subsection;

(ii) the partner is expelled by judicial determination under Section 601(5);

(iii) the partner is dissociated by becoming a debtor in bankruptcy; or

(iv) in the case of a partner who is not an individual, trust other than a business trust, or estate, the partner is expelled or otherwise dissociated because it willfully dissolved or terminated.

(c) A partner who wrongfully dissociates is liable to the partnership and to the other partners for damages caused by the dissociation. The liability is in addition to any other obligation of the partner to the partnership or to the other partners.

§ 603. Effect of Partner's Dissociation

(a) If a partner's dissociation results in a dissolution and winding up of the partnership business, [Article] 8 applies; otherwise, [Article] 7 applies.

(b) Upon a partner's dissociation:

(1) the partner's right to participate in the management and conduct of the partnership business terminates, except as otherwise provided in Section 803;

(2) the partner's duty of loyalty . . . terminates; and

(3) the partner's duty of loyalty . . . and duty of care . . . continue only with regard to matters arising and events occurring before the partner's dissociation, unless the partner participates in winding up the partnership's business pursuant to Section 803.

ARTICLE 7. PARTNER'S DISSOCIATION WHEN BUSINESS NOT WOUND UP

§ 701. Purchase of Dissociated Partner's Interest

(a) If a partner is dissociated from a partnership without resulting in a dissolution and winding up of the partnership business under Section 801, the partnership shall cause the dissociated partner's interest in the partnership to be purchased for a buyout price determined pursuant to subsection (b).

(b) . . .

(c) Damages for wrongful dissociation under Section 602(b), and all other amounts owing, whether or not presently due, from the dissociated partner to the partnership, must be offset against the buyout price. Interest must be paid from the date the amount owed becomes due to the date of payment.

(d) . . .

(e) If no agreement for the purchase of a dissociated partner's interest is reached within 120 days after a written demand for payment, the partnership shall pay, or cause to be paid, in cash to the dissociated partner the amount the partnership estimates to be the buyout price and accrued interest, reduced by any offsets and accrued interest under subsection (c).

§ 702. Dissociated Partner's Power to Bind and Liability to Partnership

(a) For two years after a partner dissociates without resulting in a dissolution and winding up of the partnership business, the partnership, including a surviving partnership under [Article] 9, is bound by an act of the dissociated partner which would have bound the partnership under Section 301 before dissociation only if at the time of entering into the transaction the other party:

(1) reasonably believed that the dissociated partner was then a partner;

(2) did not have notice of the partner's dissociation; and

(3) is not deemed to have had knowledge under Section 303(e) or notice under Section 704(c).

(b) A dissociated partner is liable to the partnership for any damage caused to the partnership arising from an obligation incurred by the dissociated partner after dissociation for which the partnership is liable under subsection (a).

ARTICLE 8. WINDING UP PARTNERSHIP BUSINESS

§ 801. Events Causing Dissolution and Winding Up of Partnership Business

A partnership is dissolved, and its business must be wound up, only upon the occurrence of any of the following events:

(1) in a partnership at will, the partnership's having notice from a partner, other than a partner who is dissociated under Section 601(2) through (10), of that partner's express will to withdraw as a partner, or on a later date specified by the partner;

Agency & Partnership
SPARK LAW SERIES

(2) in a partnership for a definite term or particular undertaking:

    (i) within 90 days after a partner's dissociation by death or otherwise under Section 601(6) through (10) or wrongful dissociation under Section 602(b) . .

    (ii) the express will of all of the partners to wind up the partnership business; or

    (iii) the expiration of the term or the completion of the undertaking;

(3) an event agreed to in the partnership agreement resulting in the winding up of the partnership business;

(4) an event that makes it unlawful for all or substantially all of the business of the partnership to be continued, but a cure of illegality within 90 days after notice to the partnership of the event is effective retroactively to the date of the event for purposes of this section;

(5) on application by a partner, a judicial determination that:

    (i) the economic purpose of the partnership is likely to be unreasonably frustrated;

    (ii) another partner has engaged in conduct relating to the partnership business which makes it not reasonably practicable to carry on the business in partnership with that partner; or

    (iii) it is not otherwise reasonably practicable to carry on the partnership business in conformity with the partnership agreement; or

§ 802. Partnership Continues After Dissolution

(a) Subject to subsection (b), a partnership continues after dissolution only for the purpose of winding up its business. The partnership is terminated when the winding up of its business is completed.

§ 803. Right to Wind Up Partnership Business

(a) After dissolution, a partner who has not wrongfully dissociated may participate in winding up the partnership's business, but on application . . . may order judicial supervision of the winding up.

(b) The legal representative of the last surviving partner may wind up a partnership's business.

(c) A person winding up a partnership's business may preserve the partnership business or property as a going concern for a reasonable time, prosecute and defend actions and proceedings . . .

§ 804. Partner's Power to Bind Partnership After Dissolution

Subject to Section 805, a partnership is bound by a partner's act after dissolution that:

(1) is appropriate for winding up the partnership business; or

(2) would have bound the partnership under Section 301 before dissolution, if the other party to the transaction did not have notice of the dissolution.

§ 806. Partner's Liability to Other Partners After Dissolution.

(a) Except as otherwise provided in subsection (b) and Section 306, after dissolution a partner is liable to the other partners for the partner's share of any partnership liability incurred under Section 804.

(b) A partner who, with knowledge of the dissolution, incurs a partnership liability under Section 804(2) by an act that is not appropriate for winding up the partnership business is liable to the partnership for any damage caused to the partnership arising from the liability.

Agency & Partnership
SPARK LAW SERIES

ARTICLE 10. LIMITED LIABILITY PARTNERSHIP

§ 1001. Statement of Qualification

(a) A partnership may become a limited liability partnership pursuant to this section.

(b) The terms and conditions on which a partnership becomes a limited liability partnership must be approved by the vote necessary to amend the partnership agreement . . .

(c) After the approval required by subsection (b), a partnership may become a limited liability partnership by filing a statement of qualification. The statement must contain:

(1) the name of the partnership;

(2) the street address of the partnership's chief executive office and, if different, the street address of an office in this State, if any;

(3) if the partnership does not have an office in this State, the name and street address of the partnership's agent for service of process;

(4) a statement that the partnership elects to be a limited liability partnership; and

(5) a deferred effective date, if any.

(d) The agent of a limited liability partnership for service of process must be an individual who is a resident of this State or other person authorized to do business in this State.

(e) The status of a partnership as a limited iability partnership is effective on the later of the filing of the statement or a date specified in the statement. The status remains effective, regardless of changes in the partnership, until it is canceled pursuant to Section 105(d) or revoked pursuant to Section 1003.

(f) The status of a partnership as a limited liability partnership and the liability of its partners is not affected by errors or later changes in the information required to be contained in the statement of qualification under subsection (c).

(g) The filing of a statement of qualification establishes that a partnership has satisfied all conditions precedent to the qualification of the partnership as a limited liability partnership.

§ 1002. Name

The name of a limited liability partnership must end with "Registered Limited Liability Partnership", "Limited Liability Partnership", "R.L.L.P.", "L.L.P.", "RLLP," or "LLP".

Agency & Partnership
SPARK LAW SERIES

# INDEX

A

Actual Authority 18
Affirmance 25
Apparent Authority 19

C

Contract Liability 15
Crimes 14

D

Direct Liability 15
Disclosed Principals 18
Dissociation 48
Dissolution 51
Duties of Loyalty 27, 28
Duties Owed by Agent to Principal 27
Duty Not To Use Confidential Information 28
Duty of Accounting 43
Duty of Care 30
Duty of Exclusivity 44
Duty to Account for All Profits 28
Duty to Indemnify 31
Duty to Not Act as an Adverse Party 29
Duty to Not Compete 29, 43

E

Expulsion 48

F

Fiduciary Duties 30
Fiduciary Duties in Agency 27
Fiduciary Duties in Partnership 43
Franchises 10

Agency & Partnership
SPARK LAW SERIES

I

Independent Contractor 3
Inherent Authority 22
Intentional Torts 14

J

Judicial Dissociation 49
Judicial Dissolution 51

M

Management and Authority to Bind 45
Master-Servant Relationship 7
Mutual consent 1

P

Partially Disclosed Principal 18
Power to Dissociate 49
Principal-Agent 3
Principal-Agent Relationship 16

R

Ratification 25
Respondeat Superior 5
RUPA 37

S

scope of employment 12
Scope of Employment 12
scope of his employment 5
Special Agents 17

Agency & Partnership
SPARK LAW SERIES

T
Tort Liability 4

U
Undisclosed Principal 18

Agency & Partnership
SPARK LAW SERIES

For a full catalog of our books,

please visit our website

www.mclarenpublishing.com